Before the Wedding

Before the Wedding

Look Before You Leap

Michael E. Cavanagh

Westminster/John Knox Press
Louisville, Kentucky

Book design by Drew Stevens

Cover design by Aavidar Design

First edition

Published by Westminster/John Knox Press
Louisville, Kentucky

This book is printed on acid-free paper that meets the American National Standards Institute Z39.48 standard. ∞

PRINTED IN THE UNITED STATES OF AMERICA
9 8 7 6 5 4 3 2

Library of Congress Cataloging-in-Publication Data

Cavanagh, Michael E.
  Before the wedding : look before you leap / Michael E. Cavanagh. —
1st ed.
      p.   cm.
  Includes bibliographical references.
  ISBN 0-664-25440-3 (alk. paper)

  1. Marriage.   I. Title.
HQ734.C394 1994
306.8′1—dc20
                                                      93-32902

Contents

Introduction

People who expect to be reasonably happy in marriage must seriously prepare for it. While this is obvious in one sense, in another sense it is *not* obvious. The person who directly prepares three to five years for state board examinations in his or her profession may spend little if any time directly preparing for marriage. In fact, many couples spend much more time preparing for their wedding (a one-day event) than they do for their marriage (a lifelong commitment). Dating, courting, or even living together does not constitute preparing for marriage, any more than playing the piano daily necessarily prepares a person to give a concert. People who seriously expect to do well in their marriage need to do a good deal of preparation. Marriage will not just "come" to them, any more than a complicated piece of music will just "come" to a pianist.

This book is about preparing for marriage in ways that will set a solid foundation to a lifelong commitment. The subtitle, *Look Before You Leap,* establishes the theme of this book. *Look* means that it's important to take a 360-degree look at the terrain of marriage. Couples who take a good look—examining both the positive and negative aspects of themselves, their partners, their relationship, and marriage as an institution—are better prepared to enter marriage than those who don't. Couples who want to see only the positive parts of the terrain are likely to get lost or ambushed after reality asserts itself.

Before means the most important time to look at yourself, your partner, your relationship, and the institution of marriage is before embarking on marriage. Couples often have more time, energy, and motivation to work directly on their relationship before marriage than after. Moreover, difficulties in the premarital relationship often have shallow roots and can be addressed without much effort. After marriage, couples often get bogged down with other concerns (earning a living, progressing in a career or careers, buying a home, having children) and lack both the focus and motivation to address difficulties that are becoming more crystalized with each passing day.

You means YOU. *You* are totally responsible for your side of the relationship. You (not your partner or parents or friends) are responsible for looking carefully at the terrain, for asking the right questions, confronting the issues, being honest and open, following your best judgment, and assuring that your needs are reasonably fulfilled and your rights respected.

Some people enter marriage with one or more relatively serious reservations but disavow responsibility for resolving them before marriage ("Tom says he doesn't have a drinking problem, so I'll just have to trust him." "Mary treats me like she's my mother, but I'm sure that'll change after we're married."). These people are asking for trouble. When problems arise in these areas, the partners will protest: "It's not *my* fault! It's my husband's (wife's) fault!"

Leap means that marriage is a transition, and it is a big transition for most people, including those who've lived together before marriage. These questions need to be addressed:

How *far* is the leap for me? Have I had sufficient practice at leaping (that is, making good transitions in life) that I'm confident that I can successfully handle this one? Or have I avoided taking any real leaps in my life (leaving home, starting jobs, entering significant relationships), so in all honesty I don't know how I'll handle it? Or is my track record of leaps not very promising up to this point?

Is the leap going to land me in a beautiful place—somewhere better than where I'm standing now, a place where I can continue to grow, if not flourish—or is it going to land me in mire where I'll become stuck and unhappy?

As in most difficult endeavors, marriage requires a good deal of direct and indirect preparation and, when the preparation is solid, research indicates that it can have measurable effects.

Assumptions

This book is based on six assumptions:

1. A fulfilling marriage requires both partners to have a basic but significant understanding of themselves, each other, their relationship, and the nature of marriage. These understandings require much honest introspection and communication.

2. Marriage requires not only that a couple have some basic understandings but also that they possess the *skills* (marital arts) to relate with each other in a relationship that will be close, continuous, and lifelong. These skills can be learned, more by some than by others.

3. Happiness is not the goal of marriage. The goal of marriage is the psychological, social, and spiritual growth of the couple and, when this is occurring, both happiness and sadness can be the by-products.

4. Preparing for marriage is likely to be both fun and painful. It can be fun because it involves two people who love each other and are working to make their relationship even stronger and more rewarding. It can be painful because honest introspection and communication may reveal information that causes embarrassment or even evokes anxiety. Part of good marriage preparation is to assimilate this information so that it becomes mutually beneficial.

5. A couple who takes marriage preparation seriously can accomplish a lot before marriage. A marriage can be a catalyst that motivates people to address things in themselves, each other, and life in general that they otherwise would have missed, ignored, or put on the back burner.

6. A correlation exists between being a fulfilled spouse and a fulfilling parent. Most people who marry eventually have one or more children, and couples need to build a healthy marriage so that their children can enter and live in a nourishing environment.

The Book

You will find this book easy to read. Each theoretical point is followed by a real-life example to illustrate it. Because a great deal of information is packed into each page, you will get more out of the book if you read bite-sized portions and digest each one thoroughly before you go to the next section.

At the end of each chapter, you will find *Questions for Thought and Discussion* to help you examine your own thoughts on the chapter and share them with your partner, if you wish.

At the end of this book are two appendixes. Appendix A discusses how couples who are planning a church wedding can get the most out of their marriage preparation visits with the minister. Appendix B explains to ministers how they can be of the greatest help to couples about to be married. You are encouraged to read Appendix B, as well as Appendix A, so that you can better understand your minister's role.

Finally, it is important to understand that no one is a perfect candidate for marriage. If you are honest with yourself, you will find areas—perhaps many of them—that you'll need to strengthen. This is normal and to be expected. You will have your whole marriage in which to strive toward perfection and even then you won't reach it. For now, you can learn some things about yourself, your partner, and marriage that can increase your readiness to make a decision that may well be the most important one of your life.

CHAPTER 1

Motives for Getting Married

Like all important decisions, the decision to marry is never based on just one reason ("I want to marry Jim because I love him."), but on several reasons, some of which are probably unconscious. Moreover, the reasons for getting married set the foundation for much of what occurs in the marriage. For example, if a man marries primarily to have a ready supply of attention for the rest of his life, and the woman marries primarily to become a mother to a house full of children, serious conflicts are likely to arise early in the marriage. Therefore, it's important to focus on both the superficial and deeper reasons for wanting to get married. This chapter discusses some of the basic characteristics of motives for marrying, as well as some questionable and constructive motives.

Characteristics of Motives

Motives have several characteristics. They can be conscious or unconscious. Motives tend to remain conscious when they are consistent with a person's self-concept. Motives that would contradict the person's self-concept of being good (reasonable, mature, unselfish) get shunted out of awareness but nevertheless remain present. For example, almost everyone who gets married will say (to themselves and others) that they are marrying to share love with their partner for life. It's unlikely that anyone would say (to themselves or others) that he or she is getting married to be taken care of financially, psychologically, or both. The latter motives, if present, would be unconscious because they are likely to be contrary to the person's self-concept.

Motives are determined by many factors. Important decisions in life are rarely, if ever, based on only one motive. In deciding to marry, many complex motives, both conscious and unconscious, interact with each other. Consequently, it's likely that every marriage contains helpful and unhelpful motives, as well as conscious and unconscious ones.

Any important life decision is unlikely to be based on a single, pure motive for several reasons. First, motives carry different weights in a decision. For example, one man wants to marry primarily because he genuinely loves his girlfriend but also because he wants someone to take care of him. While this is not an ideal combination of motives, his genuine love is predominant. However, if the relative strengths of the motives are reversed, problems may arise later in the marriage.

Second, motives can change. If a man's predominant motive for marrying is that he's found an excellent servant and his girlfriend enjoys being an excellent servant, no tension will arise in this area. However, after a few years of marriage the man's motive may change; he may now want a wife who is confident, independent, and challenging. Or the woman may no longer wish to be a servant. When motives change, significant tensions are likely to develop.

Third, motives may be either helpful or unhelpful. This means that some motives will add to the peace and closeness of the couple, while others will create tension and distance. Because human beings are imperfect, their motives for undertaking any important decision are likely to be mixed, and this includes the decision to marry. Because couples cannot expect to have 100 percent pure motives for getting married, those who do best in marriage are as aware of their less perfect motives as they are of their more perfect ones.

Unhelpful motives will be discussed first and in greater detail because they are likely to be less conscious and potentially more damaging.

Unhelpful Motives

Some motives are present to one degree or another in every love relationship and can act as a wedge instead of a bridge between the couple. As you read and discuss the ten motives that follow, the question is not: "Do *we* have any of these motives present in our relationship?" Rather, ask yourselves: "Which motives (or similar motives) are present, and how do we plan to work on them?"

1. *The need to feel adequate.* In this situation, a person feels a deep, mostly unconscious sense of inadequacy and is looking for a partner who will not only erase this feeling but also will turn it into a sense of adequacy or even superiority.

Mary is a good example of this. Through a combination of events, which she accurately or inaccurately perceived, Mary came to believe that she was unattractive, clumsy, bad, or all of the above. Because this image was painful, she repressed it, burying it in the deepest recesses of her mind. Although she grew into a reasonably attractive young woman who studied hard and did well in school, she always had an "ugly little girl" inside of her. In her early twenties, she met Tom, who was attractive, intelligent and sophisticated—all the things her "ugly little girl" wasn't. In fact, this was a major element in her attraction to Tom. By some kind of magic, Mary received from Tom what she felt she lacked. Mary now felt that she couldn't be *that* ugly or Tom would never have fallen in love with her.

The problem is that Mary deeply needs Tom to make her feel attractive and intelligent. She discovered early in their relationship that when she pleases Tom, he makes her feel absolutely beautiful and prized. But when she displeases him, he makes her feel ugly and unimportant. Therefore, she instinctively does what pleases Tom and refrains from doing what displeases him.

However, in the process she does a good deal of damage to herself, Tom, and their relationship. By submerging some of her own needs, thoughts, and feelings, she deprives herself of a good deal of need fulfillment, growth, and happiness. As a result, she becomes increasingly depressed and irritable. The more she feels this way, the more displeasing she becomes to Tom, and the process creates a vicious circle. She meets neither her needs nor Tom's, and she can't identify the problem because all this is unconscious. All she knows is that she loves Tom very much, and Tom loves her very much but both of them are becoming increasingly unhappy.

In summary, Mary should not marry anyone until she has a sense of self-acceptance that isn't dependent on anyone. It may be that Mary and Tom are going to need professional help to resolve their problem. Mary may need counseling to help her achieve a sense of self-worth independent of Tom and to free her to become "her own woman" in the relationship. Tom may need professional help to understand how he has been controlling Mary in ways that are damaging to both of them. However, if Tom does not want to relinquish the control that Mary has given him, the relationship could be in serious trouble.

2. *The need to avenge lost battles.* This situation occurs when a person has some unfinished battles left over from childhood and adolescence and needs to win them in the dating relationship. For example, Frank has a strict and possessive mother and a passive, docile father. In many senses, he loves them very much and appreciates all they did for him. Deep down, however, he feels a sense of resentment because he believes his mother emasculated him and his father.

He once told a friend that his mother acted like a drill sergeant and treated him and his father like raw recruits. After twenty years, Frank is unconsciously looking for a woman with whom he can avenge the losses he and his father suffered at the hands of this mother. Consciously, he looks for a woman who is attractive, loving, and intelligent, but unconsciously he wants someone he can treat just as his mother treated him and his father and thus get revenge for both of them.

He meets Nancy during a summer job, and over a year, they fall madly in love. Frank is on his best behavior during their early courtship, and things go very well. However, gradually and subtly, Frank begins to imitate his mother. His suggestions on how Nancy can do things better gradually turn into criticisms that gradually become scoldings. His willingness to share power in the relationship also changes; he declares he will assume power in things he knows more about than Nancy, which to him means assuming total control of their relationship.

All this is done in the spirit of making the relationship a smooth-functioning unit. When Nancy protests, Frank becomes the drill sergeant and Nancy the raw recruit. Frank has started a program of avenging his and his father's losses to his mother.

Nancy is in a no-win situation. If she acquiesces to Frank, she loses her sense of identity and the ability to have her own needs met. If she fights for her selfhood and rights, Frank will simply call in more artillery and demolish her. Eventually, she has only three choices: to be destroyed, to leave the relationship, or to get professional help for herself and Frank. The goal is for Frank to recognize his agenda and for Nancy to realize how she is instrumental in Frank's success with it, so that the whole basis of the relationship can change.

3. *The need to get a favorite need met.* In this situation, each partner has a top priority need and manipulates the other into meeting it.

Sandra has a strong, unconscious need to feel worthwhile. Growing up, she was allowed to feel attractive and popular but seldom felt that people took her seriously. She was pretty and fun, but that was about it. People did not really listen to her ideas, ask her advice, or share important things with her. Deep down, she feels shallow, superficial, and stupid.

Bill has a strong, unconscious need to feel accepted, especially by his male friends. During his childhood and adolescence, he never felt like "one of the guys" no matter how hard he tried. As a result, he felt that something was wrong with him—something that could be righted only by being accepted as an equal by a group of guys that he respected.

When Sandra met Bill, she was attracted to his good looks and intelligence, but on the deepest level she was attracted to how important he made her feel. He respected her ideas, asked her for advice, and, more important, often followed it. While Bill was attracted to Sandra's good looks and outgoing personality, on the deepest level he was attracted to the freedom she allowed him to spend time with his male friends.

As Sandra and Bill grew closer, an unconscious contract evolved. Sandra's part read: "As long as you make me feel worthwhile, I'll allow you all the freedom you want." Bill's part of the contract read: "As long as you allow me the freedom I want, I'll make you feel worthwhile." During their courtship and the honeymoon period of their marriage, the contract worked well. Both kept their part of the deal, and both were happier than they had ever been.

However, soon Sandra and Bill had a baby, and Sandra began to miss Bill's presence at home. She felt increasingly alone and overburdened. Eventually, she felt less important because, if she was as important as Bill said she was, why didn't he want to be with her? As the intensity of her feelings increased, she exerted on Bill to stay home. Bill began to feel guilty when he was out with his friends and to feel resentful toward Sandra. Finally, Sandra's mild requests for Bill to remain home on weekends escalated to statements such as: "Bill, don't you think it's about time you grew up and began to take your marriage and fatherhood seriously instead of hanging around your adolescent friends?" This sparked retaliatory statements from Bill: "Well, if you had friends of your own and knew how to take care of the baby like the wives of all my friends, this wouldn't even be an issue."

When the dynamics reached this stage, the unspoken contract on which the marriage was based not only had been broken by each partner but also had been revised. Sandra's now read: "The less worthwhile you make me feel, the less freedom I'm going to allow you." Bill's read: "The less freedom you allow me, the more I'm going to make you feel like a worthless wife and mother."

Yet, because this contract is unconscious, neither Bill nor Sandra truly realizes the nature or depth of the problem. Sandra simply complains: "Bill never wants to stay home." Bill responds: "Sandra is overpossessive." As the hurt and resentment continue to build, the stage is set for more and more behavior that will be destructive to both their marriage and parenting.

4. *The need to gain a parent for life.* With this motive, the person is looking for a spouse who is an extension of his or her parent. In other words, a man is really looking for a mother, and a woman is really looking for a father. For example, this motive may be seen in a man who becomes so dependent on mother love that he wants to have it for life, or in a woman who didn't experience sufficient father love and wants to experience it for the first time.

Stan was so enveloped by his mother's love that the need for mothering became a habit. He was looking for a woman who was unconditionally loving and always available for nurturing, who always took his side in conflicts, who always made his life as stress-free as possible, and who never confronted him with reality or made any substantive demands on him.

Alicia filled the bill for him. She also had "a great mother" and came to believe that women demonstrated their love through nurturing. Because of their strong, complementary needs, Stan and Alicia hit it off immediately.

On a superficial level, it is a relationship made in heaven; neither could be happier. However, a parent–child dynamic is clearly the relationship's basis. This dynamic can be seen in the diagram below:

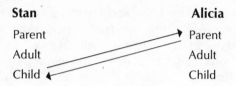

Stan	Alicia
Parent	Parent
Adult	Adult
Child	Child

As long as Stan and Alicia remain in this parent–child mode, they will have little conflict. However, this relationship has several real and potential problems. For one, very little growth can occur for Stan or Alicia as individuals or as a couple as long as Stan chooses to remain a little boy and Alicia chooses to act as his mother.

Second, Stan and Alicia cannot relate on a level of genuine intimacy as long as they remain in a parent–child relationship. Intimacy demands a maturity that is manifested by an honesty, independence, and objectivity not present in most mother–son relationships.

Finally, because Stan psychologically views Alicia as his mother and Alicia sees Stan as her son, sexual relations are likely to be ambivalent, if not filled with conflict. Sometimes this problem is resolved by the man looking for sex with "a real woman" and the woman looking for sex with "a real man" outside of the relationship.

If this couple were to marry and have children, another problem would arise; a classic case of sibling rivalry would develop between Stan and their children. The child, in a very real sense, would steal Stan's "mother" away from him. Hence, the competition would become fierce. Stan is unlikely to win this competition because Alicia now has a real baby to mother, and the baby needs her much more than Stan does. The result is that conflicts will arise between Stan and Alicia "over nothing," and he will withdraw more and more into himself or his work, feeling resentment toward his wife and the baby (the winner of the sibling rivalry).

If either Stan or Alicia begins to mature but the other

doesn't, conflicts will inevitably arise. For example, if over time Alicia gets the majority of her mothering needs met, she may want to grow in intellectual, emotional, social, or occupational areas. She may develop to a point where she doesn't mind mothering her children but increasingly resents having to mother Stan. In other words, she is growing into the adult state while Stan either remains where he's always been or regresses even further into the child state, as the diagram shows:

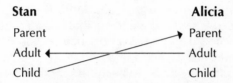

Stan	**Alicia**
Parent	Parent
Adult	Adult
Child	Child

The vectors in the diagram are no longer parallel but intersecting, which means a good deal of tension will result in the relationship. When this occurs, the relationship is at a precarious place. Either Stan will choose to join Alicia in her growth so that eventually they will interact on the adult–adult level, or Alicia will regress "for the sake of the relationship," or things will remain the same (Stan at the child state and Alicia at the adult state), which will result in chronic tension.

It should be pointed out that Stan may not appear to be a "momma's boy"—he may be a steelworker, a professional football player, or an army officer.

5. *The need to have sex.* Especially for people who refrain from sex before marriage, the need to have sex can be a very powerful motive for marriage. When this motive is strong, several problems can arise, particularly after the wedding.

For instance, Fred assumes that his girlfriend, Rita, is as sexual as he is and will match his sexual ardor on their wedding night. If this fails to occur and doesn't occur even later in the marriage, Fred can feel a deep resentment that stems both from not getting his sexual needs adequately met and from feeling double-crossed.

A second problem that Fred might experience is that, even if Rita does match his sexual ardor, sex may "become old" after a while, and they will have nothing of substance on which to base the marriage. As sex becomes less erotic, Fred may begin to perceive negative qualities in Rita that were hidden from view by the sexual passion of the relationship.

Finally, because sex is a predominant motive for Fred, he relates to Rita more as the object of short-term gratification rather than long-term love. When he's sexually aroused, he is very attentive, warm, and kind. But, as soon as his sexual need is satisfied, he treats Rita like an ordinary roommate on good days and as a nuisance on bad ones.

6. *The need to become a parent.* In this situation, the person's ultimate goal is to become a mother or a father and not to be a wife or a husband.

All that Susan ever wanted was to be a mother. No matter what else she did, she had only one goal—to have a baby. Because women don't just go out and become mothers, Susan had to get married first. But even when she was looking for a suitable husband, the main criterion was how good a father he would be.

Finally, Susan finds Bill, gets married and gets her wish—a baby. However, even as she gets her wish, conflicts begin to arise in the marriage. Susan viewed and treated Bill as a means to an end. But, now that she has her baby, she reassigns Bill's role. He had been a temporary husband—long enough for Susan to become a mother—but now she wants him to be only a full-time father. While Bill wants to be a father, he never realized that his role as husband was temporary.

A second problem is that the baby is *Susan's* baby, not *Bill's* baby or *their* baby. Susan makes this clear from the beginning. To her, Bill's role is to fetch things for her as she tends to the baby and to comfort the baby when she awakes in the middle of the night.

Susan's perception that the baby is *hers* and that men know little about taking care of babies reduces Bill to something between a junior partner and a babysitter. He is not included in any meaningful decisions about the baby; if Susan needs advice, she goes to her mother. So now Bill is neither husband nor parent but reduced in rank to breadwinner and helpmate. When this dawns on Bill, he will feel a good deal of confusion and resentment.

7. *The need to satisfy a love addiction.* A big difference exists between being in love and being addicted to love. Leroy is a love addict. When he falls in love, he's on top of the world; when he's between loves, his life is empty. Right now he's in love with Diane, and everything else is unimportant—his job, family, friends, or hobbies. As a result, he lets everything go and concentrates all of his attention on Diane.

As is also typical of love addicts, Leroy is very possessive and jealous. He has found a good supplier for his love habit in Diane and does not want to share her even for a second with *anyone* else, even family and friends. Leroy will do *anything* for Diane to keep her. He will tell her anything, buy her anything, sacrifice anything—as long as she keeps supplying him with love.

Like any addict, as long as the substance (love) is of high quality and the supplier (Diane) sticks around, everything is right with the world. Sooner or later, however, problems are bound to arise in this relationship. If Diane finds a better customer than Leroy—one who can pay even more than Leroy for her love—she will begin to pull away, and Leroy will experience acute withdrawal symptoms such as panic, depression, and hatred. The more he manifests these withdrawal symptoms to Diane, the more likely she is to want to break off the relationship. That in turn increases his symptoms.

On the other hand, Diane may mature to a point where she wants more than adoration. She wants a serious, challenging, honest, authentically sharing and giving relationship, which is the last thing that Leroy wants or can give. This is comparable to offering a healthy meal instead of drugs to a drug-sick addict.

A final problem is that Leroy may become abusive to

Diane. Addicts don't take kindly to rejection. Rejected addicts, including love addicts, are likely to be physically or psychologically abusive, or both, which compounds the problem for everyone.

8. *The need to escape the drudgery of single life.* Some individuals thrive on being single or at least live a reasonably good life as single people. Others dislike or hate being single, especially as they grow older.

Judy is a good example of this. She's tired of her boring job and of coming home to an empty apartment every night. She's tired of watching television alone, tired of cooking, cleaning, and doing laundry all the time. She's stressed out by her family putting pressure on her to marry and provide grandchildren. She's frustrated by her attempts to meet men; she hates the bar scene but also hates having no men in her life. She's too tired after work and on weekends to keep in touch with her friends or make new ones. She resists all suggestions that she enroll in a course at the community college or join discussion, church, or service groups. She has no interests or hobbies that would bring some enjoyment into her life. The only way out of this drudgery and loneliness is to find a man who will marry her and rescue her from this boring and empty life.

Somehow Steve drops into her life. After a few dates, Judy is planning their marriage, where they will live, and where they will send their kids to school. Because Steve never met a woman who so absolutely delighted in his company and because he also is tired of the single life, they eventually get married.

However, after the newness of being married wears off, the personality traits that caused Judy to hate being single begin to resurface. Because Judy and Steve can't afford to begin a family immediately, Judy has to get a new job, which she finds as boring as the last one, except the people were more friendly at her former job. When she comes home from work, she has to cook and clean not only for herself but also for Steve, who is working at a second job to earn more money. Because they moved into a different area, she doesn't know anyone and is no more inclined to meet new people than she was before marriage. Her parents and grandparents are happy she got married but now are pressuring her to have a baby, which Steve and Judy can ill afford.

At least a few nights a week when Steve is working, Judy is stuck at home watching the same insipid television shows that she had watched before her marriage. As this situation continues, she becomes increasingly dissatisfied with everything. She discovers that their apartment is noisier than she thought it would be and that the kitchen is built all wrong. The bed is too small and the mattress too hard. Steve is never home, snores, chews his food too loud, is sloppy, and is no longer romantic. She is gaining weight, feels tired all the time, and is depressed. More and more she fantasizes about how good she had it when she was single and wonders if she has made a big mistake in getting married—or at least in marrying Steve.

Judy's problems are twofold. First, she never learned how to live life well. She never built resources into her life so that, no matter what happened, she could be self-sustaining and reasonably happy—with or without a man or a family. Consequently, she brought the vacuum of her prior, single life into her marriage.

Second, Judy married her rescuer, and marrying rescuers rarely works out for two reasons. Rescuers cannot rescue people from themselves—they can only temporarily rescue people from a specific situation. In other words, Steve rescued Judy from the misery of her situation as a single, but he could not rescue her from her personal misery. In addition, people in this situation marry *rescuers*—not specific people. In other words, Judy did not actually know Steve when they got married; all she knew was that he was saving her life. After this was accomplished, she gradually discovered that Steve, while a very good man, was not the Prince Charming she had envisioned.

Judy's solution is to have a baby who will rescue her from the drudgery of marriage but, when the baby only adds to the drudgery, serious marital and parenting problems will result.

9. *The need to continue a self-destructive life.* Some people have a significant self-destructive theme in their lives. They hate themselves, usually on an unconscious rather than a conscious level. Their self-hatred develops because they could never live up to the expectations of their parents and hence feel unacceptable and unlovable. Or, they were rejected by parents, siblings, teachers, or peers because they were different or didn't fit the social stereotype of attractiveness. Or they participated in behaviors of which they are ashamed and for which they have never really forgiven themselves. Or they hate themselves for a combination of the above reasons.

As a result, these people punish themselves to purge their guilt. The result is a vicious circle: the more they behave destructively, the worse they feel about themselves, and the worse they feel about themselves, the more destructive their behavior is.

Danny is a good example. Although he had at least average intelligence and was basically a "good kid," since childhood he had behaved in ways that led everyone who cared about him to say: "Danny's a nice kid, but he went and got himself into another jam." In his family, you would think his full name is "Poor Danny." He has a habit of hanging out with the wrong friends, taking the wrong jobs, signing up for the wrong courses in school, buying the wrong cars, dating the wrong girls.

Danny marries Nancy who is the "wrong girl"—not because she has something inherently wrong with her, but because Danny doesn't have the slightest idea why he is marrying her—or marrying anyone. (Of course, Nancy has her own problems for marrying Danny, who probably has caused her more grief than happiness during their courtship.)

Danny continues his self-destructive behavior in marriage—he comes home late, forgets things, drinks too much, doesn't tell Nancy the truth, makes her feel responsible for his mistakes, breaks his promises, and is insensitive to her needs—the kinds of things he's been doing since childhood.

Nancy saw these traits when they were dating but thought that her love for him would make them go away. However, the problems grow worse. With time, Nancy is less able to see anything cute in Danny's behavior and is less able to accept his apologies and pleas for forgiveness. Nancy slowly realizes that Danny's behavior is not the result of a lingering adolescence but of a deeply engrained personality trait. Until both Danny and Nancy can clearly see this and are willing to work on it, their marriage will become increasingly filled with conflict.

10. *The need to bring about a self-centered life plan.* Whether they know it or not, some people have planned their marriage and parenthood from early childhood. As they go through life, they say consciously or unconsciously: "This is the kind of spouse I'm going to have. These are the kinds of children I'm going to have. This is the kind of house and friends I'm going to have." By the time they reach a marriageable age, they have a very detailed blueprint for the rest of their lives. All they have to do is hire the contractor and workers to bring the blueprint to life.

Although she hasn't met a man she's serious about yet, Muffie knows exactly what she wants in her husband, wedding, marriage, and home. She has planned how many children she will have, the schools they will attend, and the people they will eventually date and marry. Her personality is clearly seen in her attitudes—*her* wedding, *her* marriage, *her* children, *her* home.

Eventually, she finds her man, the contractor who will help her bring her blueprint to reality. Norman is a very nice, mild-mannered guy with modest dreams. He just wants a nice wife, healthy kids, a decent roof over their heads, and a job with good security. He figures if life is good enough to give him this, he'll be satisfied.

Because he's so "average," he's not exactly what Muffie is looking for, but he's available, adores her, and has good potential. So after they become comfortable with each other,

Muffie begins her process of redecoration. She dresses Norman differently (so he makes a statement); she improves his grammar and etiquette (so he'll be more comfortable with her friends). She changes his friends (who are losers) and broadens his career horizons (so he can achieve his full potential). All this is done lovingly; Norman, who adores Muffie, quietly goes along with the redecoration of his being.

After it becomes clear that Norman, while not the ideal, is docile enough to be Muffie's contractor, they get married and have the right number and kinds of children. However, after the honeymoon period of the marriage and parenthood is over, only three things can happen.

First, if Norman enjoys his new self, he and the whole family will flourish. Or Norman may increasingly realize that his new image doesn't fit and that it is strangling him, but he doesn't have the psychological strength to do anything about it. So, he responds with a combination of depression and passive–aggressive behavior. He may, for example, drink too much or embarrass Muffie in front of her friends. A third scenario is that, if the gravitational pull of Norman's real self asserts itself and he returns to his premarital self, Muffie may react with a combination of active–aggressive and passive–aggressive behavior. For example, she may make unflattering comparisons between Norman and her friends' husbands. Clearly, chances are that significant conflicts will arise in this marriage.

Summary

In summary, it would be rare for any couple to have 100 percent pure, helpful motives for deciding to marry. Therefore, it is important to address some questions about unhelpful motives:

1. Doesn't everyone (and every couple) have *some* of these motives for getting married? Yes, it is normal and natural not only to have one of these motives present but also to have a combination of two or more present. Problems arise when one or more unhelpful motives are present to a significant degree. No one can accurately define a "significant de-

gree," but if clear traces of the motive are evident in the day-to-day relationship, it should be identified and discussed. For example, if a woman finds herself thinking (or saying) such things as "I'm not your mother" or "You're not my father," this could indicate a motive that needs to be identified and discussed.

Because these unhelpful motives are normal and natural, there is no reason not to clearly identify them in ourselves and our partners so that their influence in the relationship can be monitored. In other words, it would not be consistent to protest on one hand that these motives are normal but on the other to resist discussing them as a natural part of a relationship.

2. What if, before marriage, we see one or more of these motives present in ourselves or our partner? Do we just break up the relationship? Not necessarily. As was stated above, if the motives are present but do not seem to be creating conflict, you can just be aware of and discuss them. If conflicts in the relationship can be traced to one or more of these motives, however, serious discussions need to occur to attempt to remedy the situation.

3. What if, after a couple is married, they realize that their marriage was grounded on one or more of these motives and that current conflicts can be traced to them. Is it too late to do anything about it? Few things are too late to correct. Basically, the couple should do what a couple would do before marriage; they should attempt to identify the motives that are present and determine how they are causing conflicts. With this information, the couple can discuss the situation openly, so that concrete steps can be initiated to remedy the problem.

Helpful Motives

Helpful motives bring peace and closeness to the marriage relationship. Examples of positive motives for getting married include:

1. To have someone I trust so fully that I can share the innermost parts of myself—the experiences, thoughts, feelings, successes, failures, strengths, weaknesses, and values that I could share with no one else, or very few others.

2. To have someone who trusts me so fully that he or she can share the innermost parts of himself or herself with me in ways that build more trust and love.

3. To live in a committed relationship in which frustration, conflicts, hurts, and disappointments can occur without either of us fearing the loss of the relationship.

4. To share my sexuality—my sexual thoughts, feelings, questions, conflicts, fantasies, doubts, and hopes, as well as my body—and to be open to receiving the same from my partner as a good in itself, as well as a means of growing in intimacy and having children.

5. To live and grow in an environment that includes the potential for the exchange of gifts on a daily basis—the gifts of security, esteem, affection, freedom, compassion, and honesty.

6. To have someone in my life for whom I can make healthy sacrifices—to make happy, even when that happiness requires that I postpone or forgo one of my favorite needs, *and* to have someone in my life from whom I can comfortably request healthy sacrifices when I have a special need.

7. To have an existential purpose in life—that is, a psychosocial purpose and not just a material one—a reason to work, to suffer, to rejoice that goes beyond a day-to-day level of sustenance, *and* to be an existential purpose in life for my partner—to be the reason he or she looks forward to getting up in the morning and going to bed in the evening.

8. To have someone to challenge me to be a better person—someone who is honest and encouraging, *and* to challenge my partner to grow in the directions he or she wishes to grow, to rejoice when he or she succeeds, and to commiserate when he or she fails.

9. To have someone to commit my life to—someone whom I can trust will always be near me, sometimes at my

side, or a little ahead of me, or a little behind me—but always within arm's reach so that I can participate in the gifts of marriage, *and* to have someone who can trust that I'll always be there to share these gifts.

10. To have someone with whom to have a child and someone to share my parenthood equally in ways that encourage family growth, *and* to give the joy of parenthood to my partner and to be a helpmate in his or her parenting.

11. To have someone to grow old with—someone who, despite my beauty and ugliness, the good and the evil in me, my successes and failures, will remain with me for no other reason except he or she loves me, *and* to be with my partner, despite all the joy and sorrow he or she brought into my life—to be with him or her and share all I have until one or the other of us no longer exists.

Questions for Thought and Discussion

1. What is my strongest helpful motive for wanting to get married?

_____

2. What is my strongest unhelpful motive for wanting to get married, and how might it affect our marriage?

_____

3. What is my partner's strongest helpful motive for wanting to get married?

_____

4. What is my partner's strongest unhelpful motive for wanting to get married, and how might it affect our marriage?

_____

Summary

In summary, it is to be expected that every courtship will contain a combination of helpful and unhelpful motives for getting married. The best situation is one in which the helpful motives far outweigh the unhelpful ones, and the couple recognizes and actively works on eliminating the unhelpful motives. The worst situation exists when the unhelpful motives far outweigh the helpful ones, or the couple is unaware of unhelpful motives that are operating in the relationship, or both situations are present.

CHAPTER 2

Correct and Faulty Thinking

In many ways, how we think strongly influences how we feel, how we make decisions, and how we respond to ourselves and others. Therefore, it is important to distinguish between correct and faulty thinking. Correct thinking is precise and realistic, while faulty thinking is too narrow or too general.

The quality of a person's thinking plays a critical role in courtship and marriage. A couple who thinks correctly can avoid many unnecessary and sometimes serious problems. A couple whose thinking is faulty, or a couple in which one partner's thinking is correct while the other's is faulty, is certain to experience many avoidable problems.

This chapter focuses on examples of faulty thinking that cause conflicts in courtship and marriage.

Being "Nice" Means Making People Feel Good

People who are nice to me make me feel good, and people who are not nice to me make me feel bad. Therefore, if you make me feed bad by making me feel uncomfortable about myself, you're not being nice to me.

This faulty thinking causes two problems in a relationship. First, it prevents me from receiving honest feedback from you because I send you a clear message: "If you want me to continue to view you as nice, don't tell me anything that will contradict my image of myself. If you do, I'll perceive you as being mean, and you know what that does to our relationship."

As long as I blackmail you out of being honest with me, I'll keep making the same mistakes over and over. This prevents me from growing in certain areas and causes intermittent, if not ongoing, tension in our relationship.

The second problem with this thinking is that it places you in a double bind. If you are honest with me about my selfishness, for example, I'll punish you by withholding my love from you or by attacking you. If you remain silent because you don't want me to view you as mean, you'll feel hurt, frustrated, or confused, and these feelings will eat away at you, causing you to feel miserable.

Correct thinking holds that being "nice" includes giving honest feedback in loving ways, even when it will upset the person who receives it. In other words, nice people are nice because they genuinely care about me and want to give me information that will help me to grow. Furthermore, they are willing to risk getting a negative reaction from me to accomplish this purpose. By the same principle, people are not being nice to me when they refrain from giving me honest feedback that I really should have if I'm ever to achieve my potential for growth and happiness.

Questions for Thought and Discussion

1. What feedback would my partner give me if he or she could be *completely* honest with me without fear of retaliation?

2. What feedback would I give my partner if I could be *completely* honest with her or him without fear of retaliation?

Being Honest Means Telling It Like It Is

I'm just a very honest person and tell people exactly what I think.
If they can't handle it, it's their problem.

The problem with this thinking is that most people who indulge in it are not simply being honest but are also being hostile, which causes two problems.

First, this thinking causes me to do an injustice to myself. I may have a legitimate complaint about your behavior, but because I fire my complaint like a bullet, you are forced to protect yourself instead of calmly and seriously considering what I'm saying. As a consequence, one source of tension quickly escalates into two sources of tension. For example, if I say to you: "You really acted like a baby last night when you didn't get your way," my legitimate concern will get lost in the cross fire that will ensue. In other words, both of us will get bloodied, and my concern will never be addressed constructively.

This thinking also places you in an impossible situation. You have only two choices: You can say: "You're right. I did act like a baby last night," or you can attack in return: "*I* acted like a baby! *You're* the one who sulked all night because I picked you up five minutes late!" The first response is unlikely to come from someone who acts like a baby, and the second response simply adds fuel to the fire.

Correct thinking understands that honesty includes not only the content of what is said but the underlying motives for saying it. In other words, I have two choices: to be honest and helpful or honest and hurtful, and the latter is not really being honest.

Questions for Thought and Discussion

1. When I'm "just being honest" with my partner, are my motives always to be helpful, or sometimes is my motive to pay back a hurt?

_____

2. When my partner is "just being honest" with me, is it always done out of love, or is it sometimes done out of anger?

_____

People Must Accept Me for Who I Am

I know I'm not perfect. Like everyone else, I have my faults, but that's just the way I am. So if you want to relate to me, you're going to have to accept my faults.

People who have this attitude genuinely don't care what people think of them, or do care greatly but pretend they don't. Either way, this is a problem. If they genuinely don't care what people think about them, how can they ever enter into a love relationship? A person must care about what people think and feel to love them and be loved by them. If deep down these individuals really do care what people think about them but pretend that they don't, this dishonesty will cause them to act in ways that create grief for themselves and those who enter into relationships with them.

For example, one of my faults is that I'm often late and make others wait for me. I've been late ever since I was a child, and that's just the way I am. I've tried to be on time, but I never seem to make it, so you're just going to have to accept this as part of who I am. If you complain about it, I'll get furious at you, because you *know* this is just the way I am and can't change.

This kind of thinking fulfills two purposes for me. It absolves me of taking my faults seriously and trying to rectify them, and it allows me to treat you in any manner I wish because my behavior, like the color of my eyes, is a part of me and can't be changed. If you don't like my behavior, that's your problem, and you ought to work on it if you want us to get along smoothly.

Correct thinking holds that everyone has faults and the responsibility to work on them, especially when the faults negatively affect a love relationship. Normal people don't have faults that they "just can't help" or that are beyond rectifying. It is inappropriate, especially in a love relationship, to expect my partner to suffer from my faults with equanimity simply because I'm disinclined to work on them.

Questions for Thought and Discussion

1. Do I have any faults, imperfections, or quirks that I feel my partner should accept if he or she really loves me?

_____

2. Does my partner have any faults, imperfections, or quirks that she or he feels I should accept if I really love him or her?

_____

Marriage Will Make Me Happy

However happy I am now, I'll be significantly happier after marriage because I'll be living in a secure and loving environment for the rest of my life.

While in some cases this thinking may be valid, it probably is not for two reasons. First, institutions (marriage, parenthood) cannot make people happy. In adulthood, happiness is not a gift that someone gives us; in general, happiness is earned by handling the realities of each day in a generally effective and rewarding manner. If I'm not handling my daily realities (school, family, work, friends, and self) in generally rewarding ways before marriage, I'm not likely to handle them any better after I'm married.

People who think that marriage will make them happy believe that the good feelings of marriage will spread to the 75 percent of each day that is not related to marriage and will make it more tolerable, if not enjoyable. These individuals fail to consider that, while good feelings can radiate outward from a marriage relationship, bad feelings from not handling their nonmarital life well can radiate inward toward the marriage relationship. And because most daily realities are nonmarital, their effects are likely to be stronger. Hence, instead of marriage making life better, life can make marriage worse.

The belief that marriage makes people happy also can be faulty because both marriage and parenthood are significant creators of stress. People who thrive on stress before marriage may thrive on the sources of stress in marriage and parenting. Those who handle the stress of life less well before marriage are likely to experience difficulty handling the added sources of stress in marriage and parenthood.

Accurate thinking holds that marriage does not act as psychotherapy that solves people's problems, as a stimulant drug that makes people feel better, or as a sedative that makes people feel more peaceful. Marriage acts more like a magnifying glass, enlarging both the strengths and the weaknesses that each partner brings to marriage. Whether people feel happier in marriage depends upon how diligently they want to increase their strengths and reduce their weaknesses.

Questions for Thought and Discussion

1. How happy would I be today if I didn't know my partner?

2. How happy would my partner be today if my partner didn't know me?

_____

3. What exactly will marriage do for me?

_____

4. What exactly will marriage do for my partner?

_____

When We Marry, We Will Become as One

While we're single, it's all right to act and live like individuals. But when we get married, we're going to become one. We're going to think, feel, and act as a unit. Otherwise, there's little sense in getting married.

Correct thinking holds that married people have three lives: a personal life, a social life, and a married life. All too often, people attempt to renounce their personal and social selves when they make their marriage vows, and this is a recipe for significant problems. To be successful, married life must build on the personal and social lives of each partner. Marriage can't take the place of these lives, any more than the third story of a building can take the place of the first two stories.

A personal life is composed of a person's psychological needs; fulfilling these needs is crucial for his or her continuing psychological development. Personal psychological needs include reasonable degrees of freedom, solitude, autonomy, privacy, and leisure time.

A person's social life is composed of interpersonal needs, such as the need to socialize with friends of both sexes, to share things with them, to visit and be visited by them, and to join in social groups, such as softball teams, church discussion groups, or literary clubs.

If both partners enjoy the same kinds of socializing, that's good. But if one partner likes to play horseshoes and the other doesn't, it is not appropriate for one spouse to force the other out of, or into, playing horseshoes.

It's a damaging pursuit for spouses to melt their personal identities into an entity called "a couple," which always means assuming a personality other than one's own and often means assuming the personality of the stronger partner. Spouses should grow *together* as a couple, but not *become* a couple.

The main obstacle to married people maintaining reasonable portions of their personal and social lives is the fear that anything one partner enjoys without the other will weaken the marriage bond, if not destroy it. If these fears are legitimate, the strength of the relationship needs to be reevaluated.

Questions for Thought and Discussion

1. What parts of my personal and social lives would I like to keep after I'm married?

   _____

2. What parts of my partner's personal and social lives do I want him or her to keep after we're married; not want him or her to keep after we're married?

   _____

As Long As We Love Each Other, Things Will Be Fine

Love conquers all. As long as we really care about each other and really want to make our marriage work, we'll be able to handle anything.

The problems with this thinking are twofold. First, correct thinking holds that angelic love conquers all, but imperfect human love does not. Evidence of this is all around us. There are divorced people who still genuinely love each other. There are parents and children, brothers and sisters, and roommates who genuinely love each other but cannot live with each other.

There is no emotion that, by itself, can keep a relationship together, any more than one emotion by itself can fracture a relationship. Relationships, and especially marital relationships, are far too complicated to be kept together or torn apart by one emotion, no matter how intense the emotion is.

Second, this thinking defines love as a static state that, once locked in, prevails over all other dynamics in a relationship. Correct thinking holds that love, even genuine love, fluctuates so that at one time I may deeply love you and wish nothing but the best for you, but at another time, I can strongly dislike you and hope that you fall flat on your face. Of course, while I'm strongly disliking (hating?) you and hoping that harm comes to you, I can still rationalize that "deep down" I love you. However, for all practical purposes, none of my current feelings or actions fit anyone's definition of love.

This is why the word "love" is not a very practical one. People can literally kill each other out of "love." A better sentiment upon which to base a relationship, including marriage, is respect. Respect means that I communicate with you in ways that don't impugn your intelligence, goodness, reasonableness, maturity, strength, or mental health.

It is much more helpful to examine how much a couple respects each other than how much they love each other. A partner's theme in a marriage can be, "I love you, but you sure are stupid," or "I love you, but you're such a baby." So, while these partners may see themselves as loving, they certainly aren't respectful.

Questions for Thought and Discussion

1. Although I really love my partner, how do I tend to disrespect him or her when I'm angry?

_____

2. Although my partner really loves me, how does she or he tend to disrespect me when angry?

_____

Our Jobs Won't Interfere with
Our Marriage and Parenthood

We're going to set priorities so that nothing will detract from our marriage or parenting. Everything will have to take a backseat to our commitments to each other and to our children.

Correct thinking holds that work *will* interfere with marriage and, if both partners work, the interference is likely to be significant. It is unrealistic in today's world to think that one or both spouses can work at demanding jobs and come home with sufficient energy and peace to be effective partners and parents every evening. Common sense, as well as observation, indicate that this is true.

It is much more realistic and helpful to expect that work will interfere with marriage and parenting and to take the following precautions.

1. Limit the amount of work that you bring home. This is important because typically no work is brought home for the first six months of marriage, then just a little work is brought home; after a few years, a significant portion of each evening or weekend, or both, is spent working.

2. Limit the amount of time allotted to discussing work. Partners may never literally bring work home, but they bring home work psychologically. They think about work, worry about work, complain about work, and plan their work for the next day. While they are doing this, they are functioning neither like a spouse nor a parent, but like a worker who just happened to drop by the house for a good meal and a little sleep.

3. Take time to decompress between work life and family life. When people have no "decompression chamber" between work and home, they are very likely to bring their frustrations, anxieties, and confusions home and displace them on their spouses and children. This is understandable but destructive. It is helpful to take even a half hour to do something to relieve the residual tensions of work. For some people, this may mean getting some physical exercise, such

as walking, jogging, or doing exercises. For others, it may mean reading, listening to music, watching a favorite television program, or talking to a friend. These behaviors, even if they take no more than half an hour, can help a person to switch psychological tracks from work to family.

Questions for Thought and Discussion.

1. Have we objectively considered how much impact my job or my partner's job will have on our family time?

_____

2. What are some danger signals we'll have to look for in terms of how our jobs affect our marriage and parenting?

_____

The Only Way to Be Unfaithful Is to Become Involved with Somebody Else

The one thing I know about myself is that, no matter what happens, I'll never be unfaithful to my spouse.

Obviously, becoming involved with someone who is not your spouse is being unfaithful, but to define infidelity so narrowly is to ignore some other very damaging ways of being unfaithful.

Correct thinking holds that getting married and having children involve a commitment of time, energy, attention, and care to your partner and children. This is not a theoretical commitment but a practical one that has daily and lifelong implications. This is what couples vow to do on their wedding day. Therefore, any behavior that significantly violates either of these purposes constitutes unfaithfulness. In fact, it's possible to be very unfaithful in many ways to your spouse and never get involved with someone else. Here are some examples:

A man can become married to his work; he gives the vast majority of his thinking, feelings, time, energy, and effort to his work and brings home the tired and cranky left-overs. This man is being literally (not just figuratively) unfaithful on two counts. He is being unfaithful to his wife by depriving her of a psychologically close marital relationship, and he is being unfaithful to his children by depriving them of a present and affectionate father.

A woman can become married to her children; she becomes so engrossed in their care that she relates to her husband like an exhausted baby-sitter rather than a reasonably present and affectionate wife.

Spouses can become married to their parent or parents, to hobbies, to pets, to food, or to drink, so that less than reasonable amounts of time, energy, care, affection, and patience are given to their spouse, their children, or both.

Spouses can distance themselves from each other sexually, because they are resentful toward each other, or are "too tired," or "just not interested." To allow this state to exist in a marriage relationship is a clear act of infidelity and violates the marriage vow.

Interestingly, few people would describe any of these individuals as "unfaithful" even though they plainly are.

Questions for Thought and Discussion

1. Leaving sexual infidelity aside, how might I go through periods of unfaithfulness to my partner?

---

2. Leaving sexual infidelity aside, how might my partner go through periods of unfaithfulness toward me?

Doubts before Marriage Are Normal Premarital Jitters

Any intelligent person living in today's world has some doubts or reservations about entering into a lifelong commitment. Therefore, I should put any doubts out of my mind and move forward toward our wedding day.

This thinking is faulty because it does not evaluate the nature and strength of the doubts. The above statement assumes that *all* premarital doubts are minor, passing, and ill-founded rather than major, chronic, and well-founded.

To think correctly about doubts regarding marriage, we must honestly assess each one. For example, if a man who has been faithful to his partner for the year or two of their engagement has some fleeting doubts about getting married, this may not represent a cause for concern. However, if he has flirted with, dated, or had sexual relations with other women during this time, his doubts should be given serious attention.

If a woman genuinely loves her partner but sometimes wonders if she is marrying him more for security and to have a family than out of a deep love, this may not be cause for concern. But if she continually has one eye open for "something better" and treats her partner in a somewhat distant and demeaning fashion, then her doubts must be taken much more seriously.

It is not rare for people who divorce to admit that, before marriage, they had reasonably serious doubts about whether they should ever get married; whether they should marry that particular person; or whether their partner was ready for marriage. Yet, these people went ahead and got married because their family, friends, and minister assured them that their doubts were "normal" and should not be taken seriously.

Questions for Thought and Discussion

1. If it's normal to have some doubts or reservations about getting married, what are some of mine, and have I discussed these honestly with my partner?

2. What may be some of my partner's doubts and reservations, and have we discussed these in honest ways?

I Would Never Do Anything to Hurt Our Relationship

I'm a reasonably intelligent, well-meaning person and love my partner very much. Consequently, I would never do anything to cause a rift in our relationship.

Of course, everyone believes this to be true about themselves, but the evidence of so many unhappy marriages indicates that *somebody* is doing *something* destructive.

Correct thinking holds that we all are capable of causing problems in any relationship, including marriage. We can cause significant problems in a marriage in many ways. One of the more common and destructive occurs when something upsetting happens in the relationship and the incident is handled in the following way:

I'm upset with what just happened.

Therefore, I must determine who is to blame for what happened.

Obviously, *I* had nothing to do with causing the problem.

Therefore, *you* must have caused the problem.

So now you have two choices: You can admit that you were the sole cause of the problem or you can blame me for causing the problem.

Because you are likely to blame me for the problem, my only option is to punish you for causing the problem and blaming it on me.

Therefore, I will mete out the punishment that will be the most effective under the circumstances.

Punishments may include: not having time to help you with your project as I promised to do, or being too tired to have sex, or withholding myself from you emotionally, or deciding that now is the time to clear the air about things that I've been saving up for the past month.

To maintain your self-esteem, you must punish me in return for punishing you by using any one or more of the punishments I considered, or come up with some of your own.

When we get tired of punishing each other, we may say something like this: "I'm sorry I reacted in that way, but I had to get your attention, and I didn't know what else to do."

This spurious apology sets the stage for another round of these dreadful dynamics. People who tend to handle their upset in this way will do significant damage to their marriage relationship.

Questions for Thought and Discussion

1. How do I tend to handle the situation when my partner upsets me?

---

2. How does my partner tend to handle the situation when I upset him or her?

As Long As We Work Hard at Our Marriage, We Won't Have to Worry about Anything

Couples today don't take life commitments seriously. As soon as some difficulties arise, they get divorced. If divorced people had worked hard enough on the right things, they could have saved their marriage.

Correct thinking holds a somewhat different view. First, many divorced couples did work hard at their marriages. They hung in there for a very long time and wanted to succeed, but the time, hard work, and goodwill they invested were insufficient to save the marriage.

Second, there is a difference between saying that marriage *requires* hard work and marriage *should* be hard work. When the "hard work" part of the marriage consistently and significantly outweighs the peaceful and joyful parts, the marriage probably has a problem that hard work won't cure.

Third, no matter how good the people are and how hard they work, situations can arise in a marriage that either will not change or simply get worse. Changes can take place after marriage in one or both partners that can cause serious conflict. For example, a woman's need for psychological intimacy may awaken a few years after marriage, and her husband may be unable to fulfill her need. In fact, one of the reasons this woman chose her husband was that he wasn't interested in all the "intimacy garbage" that her former boyfriend needed. However, she has gradually developed the self-confidence and the need to share with her husband the deeper things that are in their souls, but he is unable to reciprocate.

The harder they work to rectify this situation, the more resentful and helpless they feel. She asks: "Am I supposed to stifle my legitimate need for intimacy in my marriage for the next forty-five years of my life when intimacy is at the heart of marriage?" He asks: "Am I supposed to be able to change the basic structure of my personality because, after five years of marriage, my wife discovers she needs a more intimate relationship with me?"

Two points need to be considered in this situation. First, a couple who believes that hard work and good intentions will cure any marriage problem may work extremely hard but with minimal results. The frustration and resentment growing from their efforts may do more to kill the marriage than the original problem did. Second, the sad fact is that some marriages shouldn't be saved, especially when their toxic effects seriously contaminate one or more of the children.

Couples should work hard at their marriages, but they shouldn't have to work so hard that the work itself strangles the marriage, or that the work barely keeps a marriage alive, while all the people connected with it are dying.

Questions for Thought and Discussion

1. What are we working hard on now in our relationship? If nothing, why not? Is everything so perfect? If we are working hard on certain parts of our relationship, how much progress have we seen, and how happy are we with it?

_____

2. What could happen in our marriage that would be a sign that hard work and goodwill aren't going to do the trick, and we're going to have to do something else?

_____

Summary

In summary, it is important to understand that these examples of faulty thinking are not all-or-nothing phenomena. We can think erroneously to a small degree or a large one, or in one area but not in other areas. In any case, it is important to evaluate our thinking because all other behaviors flow from it, and any faulty thinking should be dealt with before marriage.

CHAPTER 3

Growing as an Individual

It is important to distinguish between general and specific psychological growth. General growth prepares people to live life in general, while specific growth prepares them for a particular kind of life. By analogy, a critical difference exists between general physical development and specific physical skills. The physical development necessary to become a good football player is quite different than that required to be a good figure skater. In fact, development for football may seriously impede development for figure skating.

Being a good spouse and parent requires special skills, just as it takes special skills to live a celibate life well or to be a physician. This chapter will discuss five psychological qualities, all of which are necessary to become a good spouse. These qualities are not an all-or-nothing phenomenon. In other words, an individual may possess any one of them to a degree that is negligible, small, average, above average, or great. There is no way to measure these qualities and thereby make a valid estimate of marriage readiness. It can be said only that the greater the presence of these qualities before marriage, the more the marriage is likely to be a viable one.

While it is obvious that individuals can continue to grow after they're married, two considerations are less obvious. One is that all people do not continue to grow in marriage. For some individuals, marriage not only marks the point where they stop growing, but also may be where they begin to regress. Therefore, the assumption that an immature person will "have to" mature when he or she gets married and has children is not necessarily valid.

A second important consideration is that a certain amount of psychological maturity (development, integration, strength, competence) must be present by the wedding day if the marriage is going to have a reasonable chance for success. A student entering medical school is not expected to possess the knowledge of a fourth-year medical student, much less that of an experienced physician. But, a student who does not have a good deal more knowledge about science than friends entering law school is likely to run into serious difficulty from the very beginning. Therefore, an individual cannot be too casual about the nature and timing of his or her maturity in many areas of life choice, and this certainly includes marriage and parenthood.

Growing in the Ability to Handle Stress

Every relationship has stress, and the closer the relationship, the more stress is likely to exist. A close relationship presents many more areas of potential conflict, and these areas are continually present. Therefore, the ability to handle stress well is especially important in marriage and parenthood.

People who handle stress well share the following qualities:

They keep their stress slate relatively clean. In other words, they deal with stresses as they arise and get rid of them. This is in contrast to allowing stresses to pile up at work, with parents, friends, partners or self—so that one more relatively minor stress pushes the individual over the edge.

They realize that not all stresses can be handled directly—for example, the stress caused by an unreasonable boss. Therefore, their daily schedule includes stress outlets, such as exercise, listening to music, reading, writing, and talking with friends. These activities lubricate the psyche so that the friction caused by unavoidable stresses will not overheat or damage the psyche.

They accept stress as a normal part of everyday living. They react to it as they do to rain. Rain is not necessarily pleasant, but these individuals don't become angry at the rain, fight the rain, want to get revenge on the rain, complain to everyone about the rain, or think the rain is aimed solely at them. In other words, they expect a close relationship to be stressful and are prepared to deal with the stresses as they arise with a certain degree of forbearance and goodwill.

They view stress as a potential resource. They realize that stress, when it is handled well, precedes some of the greatest growth in a relationship. Stress can act on a relationship as heat acts on iron. It can melt the rough edges, burn off the impurities, strengthen the weaknesses, and fashion the iron into a work of art. They realize that a relationship without stress is going nowhere. They do not view stress as an evil to be avoided or as something that is inherently destructive to people and relationships. They are not allergic to stress but welcome the challenge and opportunity for growth.

They view stress as a volatile substance that when handled carelessly can cause them to explode. They handle stress when it arises and do not let it build to dangerous levels. They handle it carefully, communicating about it in constructive ways. They don't throw it around in a relationship or assume the attitude: "You've caused me stress; now I'm going to cause you twice as much to teach you a lesson."

When people have developed these qualities, they are in a good position to handle stress in constructive ways. On the other hand, people who haven't developed these qualities are likely to view stress as an enemy and avoid or attack it—approaches that will create problems in any relationship.

Questions for Thought and Discussion

1. What causes the most stress for me in our relationship?

_____

_____

2. What causes the most stress for my partner in our relationship?

_____

_____

3. When I'm under stress, how do I usually handle it?

_____

_____

4. When my partner is under stress, how does he or she usually handle it?

_____

_____

5. When I'm under stress, how do I usually treat my partner?

_____

_____

6. When my partner is under stress, how does she or he usually treat me?

_____

_____

Growing in the Accuracy of Your Assumptions

Because no one can know reality perfectly, we are forced to live according to a certain number of assumptions about ourselves, others, institutions, and life in general. If these assumptions are accurate a large percentage of the time, they can be very helpful. However, when they are inaccurate, they can create considerable difficulty for both the individuals and their relationships.

The following are some personal assumptions that can create problems in a love relationship:

1. Life is supposed to be fun. Some people believe that life should be fun. Their lives have been one long party and, consciously or unconsciously, they view marriage as the ultimate, lifelong party: lots of good food, sex, great discussions, picnics, vacations, freedom from parents, great times with the kids, and other pleasures.

However, as individuals mature to the state of readiness for marriage, they modify their assumptions about life in general and marriage in particular. They come to view the basic purpose of life (and marriage) not as having fun but as growing psychosocially into more honest, liberating, just, and giving people. They come to understand that growth entails lots of hard work interspersed with some fun. In other words, fun is often the dividend of hard work and isn't achieved without some investment.

2. There is only one correct way to do things. Obviously, individuals who feel this way believe that *their* way is the correct way. They view all issues in black-or-white terms and believe that any intelligent person knows which color fits which situation. Their approach to life countenances no grays; there cannot be two different but equally rational ways to perceive a situation or to solve a problem. Anyone who perceives a situation differently is simply wrong. This attitude can cause chronic tension in a love relationship.

As people mature, they gradually accept that few issues can be reduced to black or white, and that there is often more than one sensible way to view an issue. They present their perceptions as one way of looking at an issue and invite others to share their perceptions. They are willing to examine all these perceptions objectively and to admit that someone else's ideas are as good, or better, than theirs. In other words, they are more interested in an effective approach to situations than in guarding their self-esteem.

3. Love means giving people what they want. Many people work on the axiom: If you truly respect and love me, you'll let me have my way; if you don't let me have my way, you don't really respect and love me. This approach places people in an impossible and damaging double bind that can cause mutual resentment.

As people mature, they grow to realize that respect and love are demonstrated by honesty, fairness, and a concern for the general good. Sometimes these qualities in a relationship result in one of the partner's getting his or her way, and sometimes they don't. As individuals mature, they move from the position "If you love me, you'll give me what I want," to "If we love each other, we'll each place our needs on the table and decide how to meet them in the most mutually fulfilling ways."

4. Love means possessing someone. Something inherent in human beings says if we deeply love something or someone, we must have it (possess it, own it, capture it, win it). Romantic literature, poetry, and songs are filled with this theme. It is often said that a man finally *won* the heart of a woman he was pursuing and that a woman finally *captured* a man who had previously eluded her.

This attitude poses two problems. First, things or people become less interesting after they are captured, and new challenges are sought. The second problem is that, while things are possessions, people never are. When partners allow themselves to be treated like a possession, they become slaves and are no longer free human beings. On the other hand, if they resist being treated like possessions, the relationship is an ongoing conflict. Therefore, individuals need to grow in the realization that love does not mean possessing the person you love. It means allowing the loved one the freedom to grow in all the ways he or she needs, even if it means that person may grow out of the relationship. Freedom, not possession, is the ultimate sign of authentic love.

Questions for Thought and Discussion

1. One of my assumptions about myself that, in all honesty, isn't 100 percent valid is

   _____ .

2. One of my assumptions about life that isn't 100 percent valid is

   _____ .

3. One of my partner's assumptions about himself or herself that isn't 100 percent valid is

   _____ .

4. One of my assumptions about my partner that probably isn't 100 percent valid is

   _____ .

5. One of my partner's assumptions about me that probably isn't 100 percent valid is

   _____ .

Growing in the Ability to Make a Commitment

The idea that makes people most nervous about getting married is that they are committing themselves to another person for life. This fear is often appropriate in an age where commitment to anything is rare. People find it difficult to commit themselves to their studies, work, social and religious obligations, friends, spouses, and even children. When the average person changes jobs every five years, a lifetime commitment to another person can seem like an eternity.

Being uncommitted is a normal part of childhood and adolescence. Children and adolescents relate to people and things as long as they're interesting and require little effort. However, as soon as the person or situation becomes less interesting or requires effort, the child or adolescent moves on to more pleasurable, less arduous pursuits. In an era where people feel little need or reason to commit themselves to anything, this mentality can easily survive into young adulthood and enter marriage.

This mentality can be seen even when the couple is taking their vows. While publicly vowing a lifelong commitment to each other, they are privately putting conditions on the vow of permanence. They will remain married as long as they are always as happy as they are on their wedding day, as long as they get what they want, as long as tension in the relationship remains at comfortable levels, as long as no serious problems arise, as long as they have sufficient financial security, as long as their spouse doesn't change for the worse, as long as there is love, honesty, and trust in the relationship, as long as there is no infidelity, as long as religious values don't come into conflict, as long as someone much better for them doesn't come along, as long as they are sexually compatible, as long as there is no serious illness, or as long as many other conditions are fulfilled. While the fears that underlie these reservations may be understandable and even healthy, the reservations themselves create a fragile foundation for a lifelong commitment.

Therefore, to enter into a permanent marriage, an individual must have not only the hope, the intent, and the expectation of remaining married for life, but also the psychological ability to do so. An obvious question arises: How do I know I have the ability to live out a life commitment? The only honest answer is this: You don't. But this doesn't end the discussion.

How do people know if they can complete college or a job's probationary period successfully? They don't, but two important indicators can be helpful. One is the individual's track record on commitments. If the person has a history of keeping and thriving on commitments to school, work, family, friends, and courtship, then some cumulative evidence indicates the potential to keep a lifelong commitment. If the individual, for all practical purposes, has never committed to anything, or made commitments but later resented and rebelled against them, then evidence exists that the person lacks the ability to commit himself or herself to marriage, at least until the person matures further.

A second indicator for successful commitment is an individual's ability and willingness to ask for help when relatively serious difficulties arise or are in the offing. It's virtually impossible for a couple experiencing relatively serious problems to eliminate their difficulties by themselves. One of many reasons for this is that they can't be objective about themselves, their spouse, or the situation, and their deep feelings of fear, hurt, anger, guilt, or confusion—or a combination of these feelings—significantly impair the conflict-resolution process.

Therefore, individuals with the foresight to see serious problems developing and the strength, humility, and care to seek counseling are more likely to keep their marriage commitments than those who are blind to evolving problems or who, when they do see them, are too fragile, proud, or selfish to seek help.

Thus, it is important for individuals to assess their growth in the ability to make a commitment and to work on strengthening it before and throughout marriage.

Questions for Thought and Discussion

1. My history of commitment (to study, work, friends, family, partner) is

   _____ .

2. My partner's history of commitment is

   _____ .

3. The main thing that worries me about a life commitment in marriage is

   _____ .

4. The main thing that probably worries my partner about a life commitment in marriage is

_____ .

5. The things that would cause me to break off a marriage commitment are

_____ .

6. As far as seeking psychological help if relatively serious problems begin to arise in our marriage, I

_____ .

7. With regard to seeking psychological help if relatively serious problems begin to arise in our marriage, my partner

_____ .

Growing in Self-Knowledge

Because they are children, children don't think much about who they are; because they are adolescents, adolescents sometimes think about who they are but their insights often are not very accurate. However, as adolescents grow into adulthood, their self-knowledge should become more accurate and act like a map upon which their decisions are plotted and carried out. The more accurate the map, the more accurate their navigation in life will be.

As individuals mature, some important developments take place in the area of self-knowledge. One is that they become more in touch with what they will need to continue to grow and be happy. They grow in the important realization that their psychological needs are hierarchical: some needs are more compelling than others. When people don't clearly comprehend their own priority of needs, they are unlikely to have them met. As a result, these individuals stagnate and experience a chronic low-grade depression that may periodically become acute. For example, Jim never has really thought in terms of need hierarchies. All he knows is that he's never fallen so deeply in love with a woman until Nancy came along. She's beautiful, intelligent, good, mature, sensible, unselfish, liberating, a great cook, and will be a fine mother to his children. Had Jim and Nancy been aware of the important role that needs play in a relationship, they would have seen the following sets of need hierarchies. (The number in parentheses after each need signifies the other partner's ranking of the need.)

	Jim	**Nancy**
	The need to:	The need to:
1.	be successful (10)	receive affection (6)
2.	socialize with people outside the family (7)	give affection (7)
3.	have material possessions (9)	be intimate (10)
4.	do new and exciting things (11)	spend quality time with the family (9)
5.	have sex (8)	have peace and quiet (8)
6.	receive affection (1)	have a spiritual life (11)
7.	give affection (2)	socialize with people outside the family (2)
8.	have peace and quiet (5)	have sex (5)
9.	spend quality time with the family (4)	have material possessions (3)
10.	be intimate (3)	be successful (1)
11.	have a spiritual life (6)	do new and exciting things (4)

Clearly, major discrepancies exist between Jim's and Nancy's needs, many of them in important areas. In fact, Jim's six strongest needs are Nancy's six weakest needs and vice versa. Therefore, after the marriage's honeymoon period, some relatively serious conflicts will arise because each individual wants to feed the other psychological food that the partner is either not interested in or is repelled by.

A second area of self-knowledge that should be developing is an increasingly accurate picture of your specific strengths and weaknesses, and how they affect courtship and will affect marriage and parenthood. Simply saying, "Well, I guess sometimes I'm a little selfish, and I should work on that" will not be helpful. How am I selfish? Why am I selfish and under what circumstances? What *exactly* am I going to do to remedy this, and how can you be of help to me in this area? The answers to these questions should be helpful in getting an individual on the right track.

The third area of growth in self-knowledge is banishing self-delusions. In general, absolute statements are delusions. The following are some common self-delusions that create conflicts in love relationships:

I'm a trustworthy person.

I'm an honest person.

I'm a kind person.

I'm a fair person.

I'm a reasonable person.

I'm a mature person.

I'm an intelligent person.

I'm an unselfish person.

As people mature, they add qualifiers to their delusions, thus making their self-image more accurate. For example:

I'm a trustworthy person, except when I think I have a good reason to violate a confidence.

I'm an honest person, except when I think telling the truth would do me or someone else more harm than good.

I'm a kind person, except when someone is unkind to me; then I can be quite cruel.

I'm an intelligent person, except when my emotions get the best of me, and then I can do and say stupid things.

When the self-delusions of one partner interact with the self-delusions of the other partner, conflicts are bound to arise and they are certain to remain unresolved. Only when partners can say, "I'm ordinarily a kind person, but I must admit I wasn't very kind to you on the phone today," can conflicts be accurately assessed and resolved.

A fourth dimension of emerging self-knowledge is becoming more aware of your real motives in a particular situation. Individuals grow in the realization that a single motive rarely is operating in any behavior, and the more important the behavior, the more complex the underlying motives are likely to be. Furthermore, motives can be conscious or unconscious. The motive we feel comfortable with is the conscious one, and the motive we're uncomfortable with is the unconscious one. For example, a man is angry at his fiancée as the result of a phone conversation during the day. Later, he decides to go out drinking with his friends, even though he had agreed to meet his fiancée for dinner. He sees absolutely no connection between his anger at his fiancée and his decision to cancel their dinner date and go out drinking with his friends. He reasons that it's Friday afternoon, and he'd been promising his friends for weeks that he'd go out with them. Besides, his fiancée said she was tired and needed to rest over the weekend. That's all there is to it. Period.

Until this individual becomes more aware of how anger, hurt, fear, and guilt motivate some of his behaviors, he will continue to act in ways that are damaging both to himself and his fiancée.

Questions for Thought and Discussion

1. The three needs in my relationship with my partner with highest priority are

_____

_____

_____ .

2. My partner's three needs in our relationship with highest priority are

_____

_____

_____ .

3. One of my needs that is likely to cause the most stress in our relationship is

_____ .

4. One of my partner's needs that is likely to cause the most stress in our relationship is

_____ .

5. Perhaps my greatest self-delusion is

_____ .

6. Perhaps my partner's greatest self-delusion is

_____ .

7. My two greater strengths in our relationship are

_____ .

8. My partner's two greater strengths are

_____ .

9. My two greater weaknesses in our relationship are

_____ .

10. My partner's two greater weaknesses in our relationship are

_____ .

11. I'm not necessarily proud of it, but I have to admit that sometimes one of my motives in our relationship is to

_____ .

12. My partner probably wouldn't admit it, but I think one of
    his or her motives in our relationship is

_____

Growing in Freedom

Young children are typically free, but they soon discover
that freedom can get them into trouble, so they learn to
shackle themselves. It is not until middle or late adolescence
that they attempt to unshackle themselves and regain their
freedom. As individuals grow from adolescence to adulthood,
they should be gaining freedom in at least two key areas.

One, they should grow in the freedom to become honest
with themselves and others. Honesty with others begins with
being honest with yourself. This process begins with some ac-
knowledgements and ends with a question:

I know what I'm *supposed* to think and feel about this
situation.

I know what people *want* me to think and feel.

I know what I *indicated* I think and feel.

But, *what do I really think and feel in the deepest recesses
of my mind and heart?*

Here is an example:

I know I'm *supposed* to want to get married this summer.

I know everyone, including my fiancée, *wants* me to get
married this summer.

I know I *indicated* that I'd probably get married this summer.

But, if I'm going to be absolutely honest with myself,
there is no way that getting married this summer would
be a good thing for me.

This example demonstrates clearly why we don't want to reach down and discover what we really think and feel about situations. When we do, the process often requires us to act on our deepest thoughts and feelings, and this may create a stress for ourselves, for others, or for everyone involved in the situation. In the short run, it's easier to go with our superficial thoughts and feelings. In the long run, it can cause a major disaster with lifelong consequences.

Being honest with others means that I tell them what I really think and feel as diplomatically as possible at times when failing to do so would result in an ultimate injustice to myself or another. In the example above, the man has two choices: to tell his fiancée his deep and clear belief that they should not get married this summer, or to pretend that his introspection never occurred and continue with plans for a summer wedding.

If he takes the first option, he and his fiancée may experience a great deal of stress, but at least the result will be based on honesty, and they will have no further surprises. If he takes the second option, both he and his fiancée will avoid the acute stress that honesty would create, but one of three things is likely to happen: He will call off the wedding at the last minute; he will go through the wedding ceremony but will question the validity of his consent to marry; or he will regret after the ceremony that he didn't pay attention to the voices deep within him ("I *knew* it was a mistake to get married, but I stupidly went ahead, hoping things would turn out all right in the end."). Of course, it's possible that a happier resolution could occur. However, it's risky to expect that it will.

Honesty with yourself and your partner can be compared with swabbing a wound with alcohol. It stings for a while, but it cleanses the wound of impurities and begins the healing process.

A second area of freedom is growing in autonomy. Autonomy is often misunderstood. Autonomy means that someone becomes his or her own person, stands on his or her own feet, has his or her own set of thought-out beliefs and values, and possesses the confidence to act upon them. It does not mean that an individual is selfish, listens to no one, or needs no one else in life.

Becoming autonomous entails needing to rely less and less on the advice of others. After listening to the counsel of others, the autonomous person makes up his or her own mind and acts accordingly. Sometimes these actions please others and sometimes they don't; sometimes the actions are correct, and sometimes they aren't.

Autonomy requires emancipation from the significant people in your life, especially parents. Parents who trust the wisdom of their sons and daughters and who are genuinely emancipating make the process both natural and easy. Parents who distrust their children or want to keep them dependent are likely to exert a good deal of subtle or obvious control over their lives under the guise of being caring, reasonable, and generous.

This control usually takes one or both of two forms. One is emotional blackmail ("I think it's great you kids want to move out of state after you're married, but of course you know it'll kill your father."). The second form is giving gifts with invisible strings attached ("Of course, it's fine with us if you move out of state. It's just that Dad wanted to give you our home on the lake for a wedding present if you decided to live close by.").

Autonomous individuals in these situations must be willing to be perceived as callous (not caring *whose* death they cause) and ungrateful (not accepting a very loving and expensive gift). Like most virtues, autonomy comes with a price, but it is never as high as the cost of overdependence.

Questions for Thought and Discussion

1. On a scale of 1 to 10, I'd rank my honesty with myself as

   _____ .

2. On the same scale, I'd rank my partner's honesty with himself or herself as

   _____ .

3. On the same scale, I'd rank my honesty with my partner as _____ and my partner's honesty with me as

_____ .

4. The hardest thing for me to be honest about to myself is

_____ .

5. The hardest thing for me to be honest about with my partner is

_____ .

6. I think if my partner were to be totally honest with me, he'd (she'd) probably say

_____ .

7. If I were to be totally honest with my partner, I would say

_____ .

8. As far as being autonomous, I

_____ .

9. As far as being autonomous, my partner is

_____ .

10. The one area in which I could be more autonomous is

_____ .

11. The one area in which my partner could be more autonomous is

_____ .

CHAPTER 4

Growing as a Couple

It would be rare for a couple to experience authentic love in the early stages of their relationship. No matter how long they are married, no couple attains a love that is perfectly authentic—that is, devoid of all selfishness and impurities. Therefore, one of marriage's basic purposes is to grow continually in the direction of authentic love, although many obstacles make this endeavor difficult.

Thus, it is important for couples who are planning to marry to have love goals and some way of assessing their progress toward these goals. This chapter discusses five love goals that are basic to courtship and marriage.

Growing from Romantic to Realistic Love

Maturing love grows in the direction of a more accurate perception of yourself, your partner, and the love relationship. As these perceptions become more accurate, the couple is better prepared to handle reality in ways that are helpful to each other and their relationship. The less accurate these perceptions, the more the couple is moving toward frustration, disappointment, and failure.

When a love relationship is based on delusions induced by romance, sooner or later the couple will accuse each other: "You changed after we got married," or "You're not the person I married," or "Now your true self is finally showing through." Although people can change for better or for worse after marriage, the changes that create conflict most often evolve as the couple's perceptions move from being romantic to realistic.

Perception of Yourself

Before marriage, you should have an accurate perception of yourself. Through the loving interactions that couples have in the course of their relationship, they can make such observations as the following:

> I used to see myself as a very good-natured, easy-to-get-along-with person. But I've come to realize that my good disposition is largely dependent on getting my own way. When I don't get my way, especially about something I really want, I can be a sullen, spiteful person.

> I used to see myself as a very gentle, kind person, but now I see that I can use my sense of humor to hurt people in ways that they can't respond to without appearing to be a poor sport.

> I used to think that I really loved people of the opposite sex, but now I've come to learn that I harbor some pockets of hostility toward them.

> I used to think that I was a very emancipating person, but it's become clear that, the more I become attached to someone, the more possessive and jealous I become.

Perception of Your Partner

A second perception that must be changed in the direction of reality is each partner's perceptions of the other. Through the day-to-day interactions of the relationship, partners can say things such as this:

> You are a very generous person, but you sometimes expect specific repayments for your generosity.

> You are a beautifully sensitive individual, but your sensitivity can turn to suspiciousness when you feel threatened in a certain situation.

> You have a great deal of insight into people, especially their flaws, but you don't seem to have as much insight into your own personality and your own shortcomings.

> You have a great love of life and people, but when you're not partying with your friends and are alone with me, you sometimes become bored and irritable.

Perception of the Relationship

The couple's perception of their relationship needs to become more realistic. As a couple gets to know each other better, they can say:

> I used to think we agreed on everything of consequence, but now I've begun to see that we disagree on at least a couple of important issues.

> I used to pride myself on how well we communicated, but now I'm wondering if we are communicating as honestly as I once thought we were.

> I used to think we shared the same values, but now I'm beginning to think that this may not always be the case.

> I used to think that we could handle any of life's stresses, but now I've found that sometimes even minor stresses can throw us off balance.

None of these discoveries, or even all of them taken together, necessarily mean that a couple shouldn't marry. In fact, the new insights that appear in growing relationships can create a solid foundation for marriage if they're properly understood and worked on by the couple. Problems arise when these discoveries are made *after* marriage and the couple begins to feel that the entire foundation of their marriage has disintegrated under the weight of reality.

Courtship is the time for couples to see the best and the worst in each other. It is the time to gradually take off the rose-colored glasses and replace them with clear lenses.

Questions for Thought and Discussion

1. As I've grown in our relationship, I've come to realize that I'm not as good as I thought I was in

   _____ but am better than I thought I was in

   _____ .

2. As I've grown in our relationship, I've discovered that my partner is not as good as I'd hoped in

   _____ but is better than I thought in

   _____ .

3. As I've grown in our relationship, I think we could both do better in

   _____ but I'm happiest about how we

   _____ .

Growing from Pseudo-Respect to Respect

Love that is continually growing moves from pseudo-respect to genuine respect, both for yourself and your partner. Respect is extremely important in courtship and marriage because it is, with trust, the cornerstone of any love relationship. While most couples would insist that they had respect for themselves and each other since the earliest days of their relationship, this is unlikely to be true. Genuine respect for yourself and your partner can only be earned in increments over a period of time.

Self-Respect

People must grow in self-respect before they can grow in respect for their partners. Growth in self-respect in a love relationship can be seen in the following areas:

Growing in honesty. I used to be afraid to tell you things that I knew would upset you because I didn't want you to get angry with me or reject me. I needed your acceptance and affection more than I needed my integrity. However, I've grown to a point in our relationship where one of my highest priorities is being honest with you, even if that means that you will be hurt and will hurt me in return. If you're going to love me, I want you to love *me* and not an edited version of me.

Growing in asserting my values. I used to allow you to manipulate me out of doing what I thought was important. Although going to church on Sunday has always been important to me, I used to give in to your request to skip church and go out with you. And, although I felt going past a certain point sexually was wrong, I let you talk me out of my belief. Now, I've grown to a point where I can stand firm on basic values while still being able to compromise on less basic values. In other words, I have to feel good about *me* in the relationship before I can genuinely feel good about *you*.

Growing in transparency. I used to be afraid of letting you see my imperfections, weaknesses, and failures. I wanted you to admire me, so I offered you a highly polished version of myself. For example, I would tell you about the A I got in English but not about the D I got in French. As I have grown in our relationship, I not only can let you see my imperfections, but also can discuss them with you so that we can work on them together. Because I can do this, I feel more authentic in our relationship as well as much closer to you.

Respect for Your Partner

The more people grow in self-respect in a relationship, the more they can grow in respecting their partners. Respect for your partner can grow in these areas:

I used to want to be in control of our relationship—to be the "senior partner." For example, last year I bought season tickets for the football season that begins only months after our wedding without telling you about it until I had bought them. I said I did this for you too so you could get out of the house and get some fresh air. In fact, I know you're not crazy about football, and we could use the money for more important things. When you learned about the tickets and got upset, I accused you of being a spoilsport who just wanted to sit home on Sundays and stare at the walls. But because I've grown a lot since then, I just couldn't see myself doing that now. I think your needs and desires are as important as mine and that we should make decisions as equal partners who care as much about the relationship as we do about our private needs.

I used to put you down when I was angry at you. I'd say such things as this: "How could you be so stupid (immature, insensitive, selfish, irrational, insecure, weak, or devious)?" I also put you down in just kidding ways. I just kidded you about your weight, your friends, the way you talk when you're upset, and other things. Because I was "obviously just kidding," you had only two options: to get upset with me and be seen as too sensitive or as a poor sport, or to swallow your hurt and anger and feel terrible.

I also put you down by teasing you in front of family and friends. I'd tease you about your new hairstyle, your clothes, your problems at work. Because all this was in fun, you couldn't confront me about the hurtfulness and inappropriateness of my behavior.

Now I've grown to a point where I can see that, in fact, I was demeaning and hurting you by these behaviors. I *said* I respected you, but at times I clearly didn't act like it. In other words, if someone did those things to me, I certainly wouldn't feel that he or she genuinely respected me. Now, when I'm hurt or angry, I deal with these feelings directly and don't recycle them by putting you down. You deserve much better than that from me.

Questions for Thought and Discussion

1. With respect to growing in honesty, asserting my values, and growing in transparency, I think I've grown the most in

   _____ because

   _____.

2. About growing in the same qualities, I think my partner has grown the most in

   _____ because

   _____.

3. Regarding respect for my partner, I can see I've grown in this area because I used to

   _____ and now I

   _____.

4. Regarding my partner respecting me, I can see that he (she) used to

   _____ but now he (she)

   _____.

Growing from Distrust to Trust

Trust, both in yourself and in your partner, is essential to marriage. It is the foundation upon which everything else is built. Trust doesn't need love to exist, but love indeed needs trust. As love increases, trust also increases both in depth and breadth. Trust is not an all-or-nothing phenomenon; you do not either trust or distrust your partner. One partner can trust another completely in some areas and less completely in others. Like respect, trust is two-dimensional; there is trust of yourself and trust of your partner.

Trust of Yourself

Trusting yourself has three components:

I'm growing in my trust for the purity of my motives. I am more confident that I'm at least as much concerned about your welfare as my own. At times I've fooled myself (and you) by thinking that my wishes were for our mutual welfare when in fact they were often primarily for mine. For example, I used to pressure you to relate with me in sexual ways, pretending to both of us that my motive was to increase the intimacy and trust in our relationship. Now, I can admit that my need had much more to do with lust than enhancing the quality of our relationship. I've reached the point where I'm more honest with myself and you regarding my motives for doing or not doing things in our relationship.

I'm growing in my trust for the strength of my commitment. I have to admit that, in the earlier stages of our relationship, I was not sure about committing myself to one person for the rest of my life. There's so much I haven't experienced, so many kinds of people I've never dated, and I do love my freedom very much. But as we've grown closer, I'm looking at commitment much more positively. It's something that I am more and more certain that I can do and I am starting to actually look forward to it.

I'm growing in my trust that I'll be a capable partner and parent. It's difficult to know how good you will be at something you've never done, and this used to frighten me about marriage and parenthood. But our relationship has brought out and tested so many of the qualities it takes to be a good partner and parent that I feel increasingly confident that I can do both at least reasonably well.

Trust in Your Partner

Trusting your partner also has three components:

As we grow in our relationship, I am more able to trust that you won't leave me. I find myself feeling less anxious when you socialize with your friends and coworkers. Increasingly, I want you to get the most out of life and to enjoy it to the fullest. I feel less and less possessive toward you and less jealous of your friends. I feel more trust that you love me and that you are not interested in finding someone who may be more attractive.

I am more trusting that you are honest with me about yourself and your positive and negative feelings about me. Increasingly, I'm trusting that the person I see in you now will be the person I'm getting as a life partner. I fear less and less that I'll discover a whole new negative side of you after we're married.

I am more trusting that I can share the deepest parts of myself, including some of my shameful parts, and that you won't reject me. I find myself taking more risks in our relationship and being more willing to be transparent and unguarded with you. I feel less that you may use my vulnerabilities against me at a later time if you become angry with me.

Questions for Thought and Discussion

1. As our relationship has progressed, I'm more confident that I can

_____

2. As our relationship has progressed, I have more confidence in you because

_____

Growing from Infatuation to Authentic Love

As courtship and marriage evolve, infatuation gradually wears thin and authentic love should begin to take its place. Infatuation is composed of romantic emotions, dependency, and sexual feelings that can be very strong and at times overpowering. These feelings constitute the rush, the high, the intoxication that is often part of dating and courtship.

Infatuation is a normal part of the dating process and serves to bring people together. In itself, it is rather harmless. However, if infatuation is the factor that motivates a couple to make a lifelong commitment in marriage, it can be very dangerous. It is comparable to a couple being intoxicated while exchanging their marriage vows. For this reason, it is important to know some of the key differences between infatuation and authentic love. Here are some important areas in which movement should occur from one to the other:

From being consumed by romantic feelings to being able to place the relationship in a proper balance. During the infatuation stage, all of life revolves around the relationship. It is the be-all and end-all of existence. Family, friends, work, and other responsibilities fade into the background and become relatively unimportant. As the partners mature, reality gradually emerges so that the relationship takes its proper place alongside other important relationships and responsibilities.

From giving to get, to giving to make your partner happy. Infatuation is tit-for-tat love. It gives so that it can get, and the shorter the time lapse between the two, the better. Giving without immediate getting creates the feeling of being used and double-crossed. As the couple matures, giving becomes less selfish and calculated and more altruistic. Giving and sacrificing become gifts rather than investments or loans.

From needing a person for survival to desiring a person for continuing psychological growth. An infatuated person needs a partner in the same way that a drug addict needs a supplier. The addict will pay the supplier any price for the drugs, will become anything the supplier wants him or her to become, will cling to the supplier so that the supplier never can move too far away, and will experience serious withdrawal symptoms if the supplier leaves.

Authentic love is not dependent but interdependent. While the couple needs each other to a certain degree, each partner is a self-sufficient individual who functions well independently of the other. In other words, if the relationship were to terminate, each partner may feel very badly, but he or she will not be devastated. The death of the relationship will not mean the death of either partner.

From being absorbed in each other to regaining individuality. Infatuation knows no boundaries—the two partners become enmeshed and entangled with each other in ways that defy reality. The thoughts, feelings, and values of the partners become so intertwined that they lose their identities and think and act in ways that may be damaging to both of them. As true love enters the picture, the partners gradually regain their separate identities and behave like two individuals who happen to be in love with each other.

From fixation to growth. One characteristic of infatuation is fixation; it focuses on the same issues over and over, never resolving them once and for all. Typical fixation issues are: "Do you still love me?" "Do you *really* love me? "Do you find anyone else attractive?" "Do you still want to marry me?" "Would you ever leave me and, if so, under what conditions?" "What do your parents really think of me?" "Why do you always have to have your own way?" "Why do you hang out with those kinds of friends?" "Why don't you change and become more like I want you to be?" "If you keep treating me like this, I'm leaving you." "I'm really sorry for what I did last night. I promise I'll never do it again."

As genuine love replaces infatuation, personal and interpersonal conflicts get resolved and fall by the wayside, creating room for a more loving and creative dialogue and a more interesting and peaceful relationship.

From unreal expectations to real ones. Infatuation lives in the world of pipe dreams. It causes a couple to expect perfection in themselves, in each other, and in the relationship. Nothing less than totally committed, unconditional love will do, and anything less is cause for alarm. As reality-based, genuine love appears, it modifies expectations and humanizes the relationship. It permits the couple to realize that courtship and marriage are human endeavors and that the imperfections of each partner will create a relationship that, even though it grows, will always be quite imperfect.

Unfortunately, our society tends to view infatuation as good. It is seen as good that couples live and die for each other, are absorbed in each other, become as one, give themselves totally to each other, are never apart, are lovesick when separated from each other, and die when the other dies. While this is all very romantic and exciting, it wreaks havoc with a relationship. Infatuation is very much like alcohol intoxication. It can make a person feel great, and it can make a person feel ill, but in neither case will the person function properly in reality.

Questions for Thought and Discussion

1. I can see now how my love has evolved from infatuation to a more authentic love. The two places I can see this growth are in

_____ and in

_____.

2. I can see that my partner's love has evolved from infatuation to a more authentic love. The two places I can see this most clearly are in

_____ and in

_____.

Growing from Denial to Responsibility

Maturing love grows from denying responsibility for personal and relationship problems to accepting responsibility for and dealing effectively with those problems. Denial in a love relationship is three-dimensional and includes yourself, your partner, and the relationship.

Denying Your Own Imperfection

Denial concerning yourself is based on a three-pronged theme:
1. There's no problem here.
2. If there is a problem, I'm not the cause of it.

3. Because I'm not the cause of it, we'd better find out who is.

Denial is an accurate barometer of an individual's insecurity: the more denial, the more insecurity. Individuals need confidence in their self-worth to admit weaknesses and mistakes and to feel capable of rectifying them. The following are some typical characteristics or behaviors that people tend to deny in themselves.

Anger. Everyone gets angry. Some people can admit it, and others can't. "When I used to be angry at you, I'd say: 'I'm not *angry* at you! I'm just *surprised* (or confused, upset, frustrated, disappointed) at the situation.' Now, I'm more inclined to say: 'Yes, you're right. I am angry at you for the following reasons . . . ' "

Mistakes. Everyone makes mistakes every day. Some people readily admit them; most people rarely if ever admit them. "When I used to make mistakes, I'd say things such as: '*I* didn't make a mistake. *You* made a mistake by not being clear about what time you wanted me to pick you up.' Now, I'm more inclined to say: 'I'm sorry. It's my mistake. I was confused about what time to pick you up and should have called you to check before I left home.' "

Selfishness. Everyone is selfish, and some people are more selfish than others. "When I've been selfish, I'd usually say: 'I'm *not* being selfish. I just think that what I want is best for all concerned.' Now, I'm more likely to say: 'You're right, I am being selfish. Let's see how we can work something out so that everyone's needs are taken into consideration.' "

Jealousy. Almost everyone is jealous at one time or another. "When I was jealous, I'd say: 'I'm *not* jealous. I just don't see why you always have to go out with those stupid friends of yours.' Now I'm more likely to say: 'You're right. I am jealous. Let's talk about it and see what's really going on.' "

Denying a Partner's Imperfections

In addition to denying their own faulty behavior, people also can deny faulty behavior in their partners. Examples of those behaviors include those discussed above and the following:

Manipulation. "I realize that sometimes my partner manipulates me. At times, he treats me more like a servant than an equal partner. Earlier in our relationship, I wasn't secure enough to confront him about this. I'd tell myself that I should help him because, 'He's busier than I am,' or 'His work is more important than mine,' or 'He'd help *me* out if I asked him.' However, now I'm more likely to say: 'Sometimes I think you ask me to do things for you that you could do for yourself. For instance, it won't be any easier for me to pick up your shirts at the cleaners than it would be for you.' "

Inadequacy. "Sometimes my partner isn't as sensitive, industrious, unselfish, consistent, or wise as she could be, but I could never admit this to myself. When problems arose in these areas, I'd blame myself for them or chalk them off to minor lapses in her behavior. As I've grown in the relationship, I'm more able to deal directly with these issues. Instead of saying: 'It's too bad you didn't get the job you interviewed for,' I'm more inclined to say: 'I'm sorry you didn't get the job, but I think you're not preparing for these interviews nearly as much as you should.' "

Dishonesty. "My partner has been dishonest with me on occasion, but I couldn't admit it. I rationalized his dishonesty by assuring myself that he had simply forgotten to tell me things, or was confused, or he told me and I forgot. Now I've grown to the point that I confront him and help him examine the causes of his dishonesty."

Dependence. "At times I think that my partner is too dependent on some people (her mother, for example) and some things (food, for example). At first, I denied this was true, rationalizing that she was just very close to her mother or that she just loved good food. However, I've grown to see that these dependencies are not good and in fact interfere with our relationship. Recently, I've been able to voice some of my concerns in ways that are honest as well as loving."

Denying Imperfections in the Relationship

Denial can also extend to the quality of a love relationship. Here are some examples:

We used to pride ourselves on how well we communicated—better than most married couples. Now we're beginning to acknowledge that while we do communicate well on some issues, we don't communicate very well on others, such as how much social life I can still have with my friends and when we're going to start a family. At least now we can admit this, which is the first step toward doing something about it.

We used to brag about how open and honest we were with each other. But, as we've grown closer, we can admit to areas of privacy that we don't want to share with each other, at least not now. We've been able to discuss the situation, and although it raises our anxiety, we are beginning to accept that we may never want those areas of privacy to be known completely.

We used to think that, even when things went wrong, we both had good intentions toward each other, and that's all that really mattered. As we've matured in the relationship, we can admit that we don't *always* have good intentions toward each other. Sometimes, particularly when we are very angry, we intentionally say and do things to hurt the other, and we hope the other falls on his or her face once in a while. While acknowledging these feelings isn't pleasant, it is honest and can help us scrutinize our motives when we are upset.

Issues Regarding Denial

Whether the faulty behavior being denied is your own, your partner's, or that of the relationship, four issues must be considered.

Denial reflects a lack of security and confidence. Denial states: "If I were to admit that this threatening reality exists, I, my partner, and the relationship would be in trouble because we lack the courage and love to deal with it effectively."

Denying unpleasant reality is directly comparable to pretending that one room of a mansion is not on fire. The people in the mansion assure themselves and each other: "I don't smell smoke, do you?" or "I do smell smoke, but it must be coming from outside," or "There's a fire in one of the rooms, but our mansion is so big and beautiful that we can easily tolerate a little fire." The problem is that sooner or later the fire will gradually spread to the other rooms. Or one day spontaneous combustion will cause the mansion to explode in flames and destroy the entire mansion.

To the extent that denial exists in any or all dimensions of a relationship, the partners are not really marrying each other. They are only marrying the parts that they allow themselves and each other to see. In other words, the edited version of one partner is marrying the edited version of the other. It won't be until after the wedding that the partners will become unedited.

It's likely that many couples are denying one or more significant issues in their relationship. This should not be accepted as "just a natural part of human imperfection," any more than a room on fire should be seen as simply a nuisance. As much as possible, pockets of denial should be rooted out before marriage and openly discussed, even if it requires the help of a third party.

Questions for Thought and Discussion

1. As I've grown in our relationship, I can see that the two behaviors I denied most in myself were _____

and _____, but now I
can admit to them and discuss them with my partner.

2. As I've grown in our relationship, I can see that the two
behaviors my partner used to deny most in himself (herself)

   were _____ and

   _____, but now he
   (she) can admit them, and we're both working on them.

3. I used to think our relationship was close to perfect, but
now I can see that

   _____.

4. My partner used to think our relationship was close to perfect, but now she (he) can see that

   _____.

Summary

In summary, several combinations of growth can occur in a
love relationship.

Both partners can grow as individuals and as a couple at
the same rate. This growth has three dimensions: individual growth, relationship growth, and rate of growth.

Both partners grow as individuals, but at different rates. In
a marriage relationship, for example, a woman may grow
nicely into the role of mother, while the man may grow
more slowly, not sure of his role and his competence as a
father. This difference may generate conflict, depending
upon the overall health of the relationship.

Both partners grow as individuals, but they grow parallel to, or away from, each other. For example, the man may grow in self-confidence as a businessman, while the woman may grow in self-assertiveness. Both areas of growth are good in themselves. However, as the man grows in professional competence, he has more responsibilities at work, and, as the woman grows in assertiveness, she begins to confront him about his increasing absence from her and the children. So, while the partners are growing as individuals, their relationship is faltering.

One partner grows, but the other remains the same or regresses. For example, a woman may grow in self-identity and confidence. She discovers new talents and interests and returns to school to develop them. In the process, she makes new friends and decides to pursue a part-time career when she graduates. Her husband, on the other hand, may be threatened by her growth and regress. He's afraid she'll find him and the family less interesting and that she'll eventually become more successful and popular than he is. He begins to eat and drink too much, has temper tantrums, and picks fights with her. In other words, as the woman and man move in opposite, vertical directions, their relationship is in jeopardy.

Both partners regress. After the honeymoon period of marriage and parenthood, the couple is faced with the fact that their fantasies about each other, marriage, and parenthood were just that—fantasies. They built dreams on sand, and the sand couldn't support them. As a result, they both become more adolescent and childlike in their behavior.

None of these last three situations represents an insolvable problem. With sufficient motivation, psychological strength, and help from both partners, all three situations may be rehabilitated, at least to a certain degree. The important point is that growth in marriage and parenthood is not automatic, and partners do not necessarily grow in concert. Therefore, it's important to be mindful of the growth combinations that can occur in marriage and to aim at the best combination: both partners growing as individuals and as a couple at the same rate.

CHAPTER 5

Parents and Friends

Parents and friends often play an important role in a couple's courtship and marriage. Sometimes their role is obvious, and sometimes it's so subtle that it's unnoticeable. However, the fact that it's subtle does not lessen its influence. Whether obvious or subtle, the role of parents and friends is often overlooked, and it can be very complex.

Relationship with Parents

Parents' Views

Most people who are courting have two living parents, although they may not have remained married to each other. Thus, each couple has four parents who have been married twenty or more years and have developed their ideas about marriage, parenthood, and their son's or daughter's readiness for it. The simplest and ideal situation occurs when these three factors exist:

1. All four parents think that each partner is ready to make a life commitment in marriage.

2. All four parents think that the person their son or daughter is planning to marry is the right one.

3. All four parents are correct; the partners *are* ready to make and live out a life commitment and are marrying someone who can successfully live out the commitment.

Reality, however, has a way of reducing the number of ideal situations. While it would become unwieldy to discuss all the combinations that can occur, it should be helpful to be aware of some of the more common situations. For example, it could be that neither person is ready to make a life commitment at this point in his or her life, or possibly will never be ready to make such a commitment. Both individuals may be ready for a commitment but are planning to marry the wrong person. It could be that one person is ready to make a life commitment while the other isn't, or one person would be perfect for the other but not vice versa. In other words, Mary may be a good wife for Jim, but Jim would not be a good husband for Mary.

Yet because the four parents don't really know all the relevant aspects of the people involved or comprehend the deeper psychosocial issues involved in dating, courtship, and marriage, they may unanimously approve of the couple's plans to marry. This approval can create a strong, reinforcing influence that unfortunately erases any doubts the couple may have about their situation: "We *must* be doing the right thing. Look how much the people who know us the best approve."

On the other hand, parents can be mistaken in the opposite direction. A mother, for example, may be overpossessive of her son (though she may be the last to realize it). Therefore, she believes her son is not ready to make a life commitment, or is marrying the wrong woman—even though reality contradicts either or both of her beliefs. A father who has experienced a great deal of hurt, frustration, and disappointment in his marriage may be fundamentally opposed to marriage (though he may be the last to recognize this) and therefore discourages anyone from getting married, regardless of the circumstances.

In each example, the parents' perceptions are clouded or distorted by their own needs and experiences.

Response to Parents' Views

So, what's a couple to do? Should they abide by their parents' feelings about their relationship and wedding plans or should they ignore them? Like most questions on complicated issues, this question is much too simple. Couples should neither automatically abide by their parents' feelings (even when they appreciate them) nor automatically reject them (just because they don't appreciate them).

If all four parents of the couple are living, they have experienced a minimum of eighty years of marriage and parenting experience. This does not mean that parents will always be correct in their assessments, of course, but it is just as unlikely that they will always be wrong. The woman's parents could have lived an ideal marriage for twenty years and still be wrong in their opinions about the couple. And the man's parents could have had a turbulent marriage that ended in divorce and still be correct in their perceptions of the couple.

The basic point is that it's important to respect the views of parents but also to understand what "respect" means. Respect means to look at something more than once—to look at it twice or ten times. For example, Jim's father thinks Jim should finish college before he marries Nancy. Jim's mother disagrees with her husband and believes Jim is capable of being a good husband, whether or not he finishes school.

Nancy's father loves to go fishing with Jim and therefore thinks he's a great guy; the pending marriage is a chance to gain a son, or at least a fishing partner. Nancy's mother doesn't feel the same way; she thinks Jim is immature and selfish and will treat her daughter more like a maid than a wife. Whose view should the couple respect? Everyone's. The chances are good that each parent's viewpoint possesses some truth.

Respecting each view does not mean *agreeing* with it. Respecting the ideas of others resembles panning for gold. A prospector realizes that the vast majority of material that lands on his pan will be sand or fool's gold, but he looks twice at each panful of material to sort out the nuggets of gold. He never takes the attitude: "Well, it looks like there's mostly sand in the pan, so I'll just dump the whole thing out and look elsewhere."

Couples have two options. They can respect or disregard their parents' views. To disregard them may well be to throw out at least one or two nuggets of gold. If the couple respects their parents' views, they should do so seriously rather than haphazardly or simply as a token gesture. They also should invite feedback from all the parents involved in the situation.

Eliciting Feedback from Parents

How a couple goes about this specifically is a matter of individual choice, but it would seem helpful to work from a basic format.

First, the couple should examine their deepest motives for soliciting feedback. Is it to gather information that they will consider seriously, or is it to get information that they want to hear? If the latter motive is present, then the couple will consciously or unconsciously manipulate the parents into saying "the right thing," or, if the parents say "the wrong thing," the couple will become defensive and argumentative ("Yes, but, you don't *really* know us.").

Second, the couple must genuinely invite the parents to give feedback; they must give the parents the freedom to be honest. The couple's attitude can be: "We'd like your impressions, suggestions, and questions so that we can take them home, discuss them, and use them to our advantage." A counterproductive invitation would be: "We want to know what you think, but you'd better think the way we do, or you're going to have a fight on your hands."

Third, it's important not to treat each set of parents as one unit, as in: "My parents think Jim will make a great husband." The enthusiasm for Jim may not be shared with equal intensity by each of the parents.

Fourth, it is helpful for the couple to have some idea of the

kinds of feedback they want. In general, a couple would want
to receive information that deals with these things:

their readiness for marriage;

suitability of the choice of a mate;

questions or concerns that the parents have about the
relationship;

areas about which the parents feel good or confident;

suggestions from the parents based on their own marital,
parenting, or life experiences.

ways the parents are willing to be helpful to the couple
and areas where the parents would be unable or unwilling to help.

Different couples may use different methods to get this information. One couple may want to go together to each set of
parents; another couple may want to go individually and talk to
parents separately; and still a third couple may find communication through writing to be the most effective method.

Some couples may object to eliciting feedback from their
parents. A couple may take the position that they themselves
are in the best position to know what they are doing, so parents would not be of any help. Such a couple has adopted a
principle that only those who are directly involved in an endeavor can possess all the information necessary to make correct decisions. If this principle were correct—and it is not—
then married people cannot learn a thing from other married
people, parents cannot learn from other parents, and teachers
cannot learn from other teachers. Because it is doubtful that a
couple would apply this principle to any area outside of their
own situation, the nature of their motivation and resistance
comes into question.

Another objection could be that the only effect such discussions will have is to awaken sleeping dogs; that is, they will
only bring up issues that create tension and resentment. The

response to this is that this *could* occur, but the issue still needs further discussion.

First, a couple that asks for honest feedback must be prepared to accept it. If the couple cannot tolerate honest feedback from parents, can they tolerate it from each other? In most cases, it can be assumed that when parents give anxiety-producing feedback, they do so out of love even though they may not always have the skills to do so gracefully. It is then up to the couple to evaluate the feedback.

Second, if one or both sets of parents have "sleeping dogs," they won't remain asleep forever. They will eventually wake up and bite the couple at a time when they least need it ("I *knew* Jim wasn't right for you but kept my mouth shut because you were so madly in love with him!"). Generally, it's better to get issues out on the table and deal with them than to sweep them under the rug and trip over them for the rest of your life.

Attitude toward Parents

Whether or not a couple chooses to discuss their relationship and marriage plans with parents, another parental issue needs to be discussed: What are the attitudes of each partner to his or her own parents and to his or her partner's parents? This area is very important because it would be rare for parents not to be a significant factor in a couple's marriage. There are two dimensions to this topic.

The first dimension deals with the attitude each partner has toward the role of his or her own parents and the partner's parents in the pending marriage. Basically, a person can have one of three attitudes:

I want you to play an important part in our lives—to be there as a resource and support and as a future grand-parent.

I want you to play a minor role in our lives. I want us to keep in touch and visit, especially around the holidays and important events. But, other than that, I'd like us to lead pretty much separate lives.

I don't want you to be a part of our lives. I want to begin a new life for myself and family and would prefer it if you left us alone.

It's important to understand that, taken alone, none of these attitudes is necessarily healthier than the others. For example, it could be that a person who harbors the last attitude has a very good reason for doing so. The issue is not so much which attitude you have, but how it affects your marriage. Conflicts will arise, for example, when the man has one attitude toward his fiancée's parents, and his fiancée has a very different one. He may view his future mother-in-law as intrusive, manipulating, and overprotective, while his fiancée views her mother as assertive, wise, and loving. The more the man criticizes his future mother-in-law, the more his fiancée views the criticism as directed not only toward her mother, whom she dearly loves, but also toward herself. She reacts by vehemently defending both her mother and herself and by criticizing her partner in return ("I wish you had some of the qualities you resent in my mother. In fact, maybe that's the reason you resent her—because *you* lack those qualities."). In such a situation, it is important for the couple to discuss these issues openly and honestly to see if at least some partial resolution can be achieved.

In terms of disliking parents (or anyone else), it may be helpful to consider some basic reasons why we dislike people. We tend to dislike people who:

Don't meet some of our basic needs. "I need to be affirmed at least once in a while, and my fiancée's mother never affirms me."

Threaten a precious part of our self-concept. "I need to see myself as quite intelligent or mature or entertaining, and my fiancée's parents don't share my view."

Threaten to take away something we want or have. "I want my fiancée's undivided admiration, but she admires her father as much as or more than she admires me. I resent her father for this and attempt to make him less admirable in her eyes."

Have values contrary to ours. "My fiancée's father respects only people who are materially successful and powerful, and I have intentionally chosen a lifestyle that is simple and altruistic."

Attempt to manipulate us into being what they want us to be. "My fiancé's mother wants me to be more religious and have a child immediately, and right now I'm not inclined to do either."

Have hurt us. "My fiancée's father 'teases' me about being artistic rather than athletic."

These dynamics most likely account for the vast majority of reasons that we dislike our own parents, our partner's parents, or both sets of parents.

It can be helpful to pinpoint the exact nature of the dislike and discuss it with your partner so that at least a first step in the direction of resolution can be taken. Even if the conflict can never be resolved (mostly because one or both partners *don't want* to resolve it), at least some demilitarized zone can be mapped out so that peace can prevail at family functions and the children can enjoy their grandparents.

Relationship with Friends

A Source of Feedback

Like parents, friends are often an issue with people who are dating or married. The issue of friends has several facets. One is that friends, depending on how honest they are, can be an important source of feedback. If they are good friends and have known you for some time, they may understand parts of you that neither you nor your partner see very clearly—parts that are important to consider. For example, Christine's best friend has seen how cruel Christine can be when she gets very hurt and angry. Christine gives little thought to her behavior after the issue blows over, but her actions leave gaping wounds in the people around her.

Andy's best friends know that, when Andy is out with the boys, he can get quite drunk, which causes him to become hostile and reckless. Christine's fiancé has never experienced her cruelty because he's always on his best behavior and is dedicated to making her happy. Andy's fiancée has never seen him drunk and is not aware that a very different side of him gets released when he has too much to drink.

It could be that Christine's best friends don't want to confront her with her behavior—or how it can destroy a relationship—because they don't want to incur her wrath or place their friendship in jeopardy. So they and Christine pretend that it doesn't exist.

Andy's friends may feel that Andy's drinking is his business and that if they did bring it up, Andy would point out their own excesses. So two "high-tension wires" are closing in on each other (Christine's latent cruelty and Andy's latent alcoholism), and it will be only a matter of time before they make contact.

The point is that close friends sometimes see us more objectively than we see ourselves or than our partner sees us. They may be reluctant to share their observations with us for the reasons mentioned above. However, a couple who is serious about their relationship and pending marriage can find ways of inviting friends to share their concerns, questions, and hopes in an accepting and nonthreatening atmosphere.

Choice of Friends

A second facet of the relationship between friends and the courtship–marriage process is that a person's choice of friends indicates to some extent who he or she is. To a degree, birds of a feather *do* flock together.

Friendships, especially close friendships, have some definable basis. Mutual needs are being met on both the conscious and unconscious levels. Friends make us feel what both our "light sides" and "dark sides" want to feel. On the light side, friends can make us feel loved, intelligent, entertaining, free, popular, strong, admired, and courageous. On the dark side, friends can create an environment in which we can be antisocial, exploitive, reckless, derogatory, intimidating, superior, irresponsible, and overindulgent.

Therefore, while it would be inappropriate to exaggerate the importance of friends when evaluating an individual's personality, it is equally inappropriate to underestimate their importance. Anyone who says, "I love Jim dearly, but I can't stand his friends" should not be so naive as to leave it there. It could be that the woman who says this simply has a personality conflict with her fiancé's friends. On the other hand, it's at least as likely that a value conflict exists between her and her fiancé's friends that she should investigate. If she feels, "I just don't see what Jim sees in some of his friends," she should find out.

Jealousy of a Partner's Friends

A third issue about friends deals with jealousy. Often when people are in the initial, less secure stages of love, they want to be the only person in the world who can make their partner happy. Everyone else who can make their partner happy (make him or her feel important, attractive, popular) is viewed as a rival and an intruder. Typically, the jealous partner will criticize the intruder in an attempt to make him or her appear less admirable and will attack the other partner for having such an undesirable friend.

As understandable as the dynamics are, they are dangerous business for several reasons. First, it is a serious assault on your partner. It's saying: "You are really stupid, weak, or evil to think your friend is a worthwhile person." While the person making the attack can deny that he or she is disparaging the partner, there is no getting around the fact that this is indeed what is happening.

Second, the partner has only two choices: to continue the friendships or to discontinue them. If he or she continues the friendships, they will be a continuing source of tension and resentment that could last for years into the marriage. If he or she discontinues the friendships, several problems may occur. The partner who has agreed to give up the friendships will feel a deep resentment that will create distance in the love relationship and at least unconsciously call for revenge. The partner who has given up the friendship also will feel a sense of isolation because of the void left by the absence of the former friends and the distance created from the partner. On the other hand, the individual who has forced his or her partner to give up friends will feel mean and guilty, at least on a subconscious level, which also will create distance in the relationship.

Third, jealousy in a love relationship often brings about the very thing that the jealous partner fears the most. Jealousy says: "I'm afraid to lose you," but the pressure this places on the partner may cause him or her to leave the relationship to find peace or to find another partner who is more liberating.

Rather than subject a relationship to these destructive dynamics, it's better to deal with jealousy in an honest and compassionate way. To do this, several things must be understood.

For some reason, jealousy seems to be the last feeling to which people want to admit. They'd rather admit to homicidal feelings than to jealousy. Yet, feeling jealous is as normal and basic as any other feeling (Jealousy is clearly present in infants.). It's natural that the more we love somebody, the more we want to possess and share him or her with no one else. We want to be the sole source of our loved one's admiration, joy, nourishment, and peace. In addition, we are frightened that the one we love may find a more fulfilling partner and leave us.

However, if there is one acid test of love, it lies here. A person who deeply and maturely loves someone wants that individual to get as many needs met as possible and, at an extreme, even to leave the relationship if it means moving to a more growth–producing situation. The reality is that no one person can effectively meet all the needs of another. Normal people need a wide range of need-fulfillers: same-sex friends, opposite-sex friends, coworkers, family, relatives, older people, and younger people. Just as one food, no matter how nutritious it is, can never meet all a person's health needs, one relationship—no matter how loving it is—can never meet the full complement of a person's psychosocial needs.

Jealousy can be a sign of strong positive feelings but also can be a symptom of a lack of sufficient trust and altruism. The lack of trust is seen in the implicit assumption that the partner's love is so shallow that he or she will fall in love with the first attractive person to come along. The lack of altruism is seen in the act of discouraging your partner from growing through any means that lie outside the relationship.

These two issues, trust and altruism, need to be addressed in an honest and compassionate manner by the partners so that both virtues can be gradually increased and jealousy can be gradually diminished. However, a final, realistic note is in order: Some people are pathologically jealous, and discussions between the partners are likely to be unproductive in these cases. In situations like this, professional help most likely will be necessary, as is a serious reassessment of the relationship.

Influence of Friends on a Love Relationship

A fourth friendship issue deals with the relationship between your love relationship and your friends. On the positive side, genuinely good friends can be a marvelous resource in courtship and marriage. They can be relied upon to give honest feedback, to keep things in confidence, and to be a source of understanding and support. There may even be times when a person doesn't feel comfortable discussing something with a partner but does feel comfortable doing so with a close friend.

However, here are a few precautions about confiding in friends. It is important not to allow friends to have an undue influence on the love relationship ("Nancy says we shouldn't . . . ") or to use a friend as a spokesperson to say things we are reluctant to say to our partner ("Tom thinks you're too possessive."). The main effect of these behaviors is to create tension between your partner and your friends.

A second consideration is that very close friendships will, or at least should, change when one of the friends begins the courtship–marriage process. Prior to courtship, close friends often spend countless hours together. They often are the most important people in each other's life—at least on the functional level—and deep feelings of affection and intimacy can develop between same-sex and other-sex friends. When one of the friends falls in love with someone, confusion and tension often arise.

Intimate friendships either change when the courting–marriage process begins, or they don't. If they do—if less time is spent with friends and the quality of the time diminishes—this can create feelings of loss and resentment on the part of one's friends ("Now that she's found Bill, she doesn't need me anymore."). If the friendship is not modified and the individual has two "equal best friends" (the friend and the partner), this may create feelings of jealousy and resentment in the partner. This dilemma has no simple answer, but it's important to anticipate it and keep the lines of communication open with all the people involved.

Another area of caution is a reminder that it's natural to compare your partner with your best friend, whether the friend is a man or a woman. In a sense, the temptation is to make your longtime and closest friend a prototype of what a life partner should be. This may prompt a little voice in the back of your head to say, "My best friend wouldn't have been so insensitive as to have said what my fiancé just said." Some cautions must be kept in mind about such comparisons. One, people who have grown to be best friends have often known each other for five, ten, fifteen, or twenty years and know each other very well. They are sensitive to each other's needs and vulnerabilities and do their best to respect them. Therefore, it is unrealistic to compare a boyfriend or girlfriend whom one has known for a year or two with one's best friend. On the other hand, if your partner is a greater source of frustration or disappointment than your friends, the nature of the love relationship should be evaluated more closely.

A second consideration is that a characteristic you like in a friend but find absent in a partner is not necessarily a good characteristic. For example, Bill loves his friends because they all go out and drink too much and have a rowdy time on the weekends. Bill criticizes his fiancée as being a wet blanket because "being wild" is not her idea of a good time. If this kind of recreation is a high priority to Bill and a turn-off to his fiancée, the issue should be resolved before they decide to spend a lifetime hurting each other.

In summary, friends are often an important part of an individual's courtship–marriage process. Ordinarily, friends represent both a real source of support and at times a real source of tension. If couples can be aware of this and have a clear picture of the dynamics of their friendships, needless conflicts will be prevented and mutual need-fulfillment can occur.

Questions for Thought and Discussion

Circle the letter that best describes your impressions:

I think my mother:
   a. strongly approves of my getting married at this point in my life;
   b. approves, but not strongly;
   c. disapproves.

I think my father:
   a. strongly approves of my getting married at this point in my life;
   b. approves, but not strongly;
   c. disapproves.

I think my mother:
   a. strongly approves of the person I'm going to marry;
   b. approves, but not strongly;
   c. disapproves.

I think my father:
   a. strongly approves of the person I'm going to marry;
   b. approves, but not strongly;
   c. disapproves.

I think my partner's mother:
    a. strongly approves of his (her) marrying me;
    b. approves, but not strongly;
    c. disapproves.

I think my partner's father:
    a. strongly approves of his (her) marrying me;
    b. approves, but not strongly;
    c. disapproves.

Complete each of the blanks with the very first thing that comes into your mind. After you've filled in all the blanks, go over them and add any second or third thoughts.

1. What I would *really* like to know from my mother about her thoughts and feelings about my partner and my getting married is

    ————————————————————— .

2. What I would *really* like to know from my father about his thoughts and feelings about my partner and my getting married is

    ————————————————————— .

3. What I would *really* like to know from my partner's mother about her thoughts and feelings about my partner and my getting married is

    ————————————————————— .

4. What I would *really* like to know from my partner's father about his thoughts and feelings about my partner and my getting married is

    ————————————————————— .

5. My main concern with respect to my mother and my courtship and marriage is

    ————————————————————— .

6. My main concern with respect to my father and my courtship and marriage is

   _____ .

7. My main concern with respect to my partner's mother and
   my courtship and marriage is

   _____ .

8. My main concern with respect to my partner's father and
   my courtship and marriage is

   _____ .

9. The two things from my parents' marriage that I hope I can
   bring into my marriage are

   _____ .

10. The two things I saw in my parents' marriage that I hope I
    can improve upon are

    _____ .

11. If my best friend were to be honest, he or she would say to
    me regarding my pending marriage

    _____ .

12. To tell the truth, I think my partners' friends

    _____ .

13. After I'm married, the friends I have now

    _____ .

14. Compared to my best friend, my partner is

    _____ .

15. My partner's feelings about my friends are

    _____ .

CHAPTER   6

Communication

Communication in a love relationship is like an intravenous feeding tube that is attached to each partner. When nutrients flow through the intravenous tube, the relationship can flourish. However, when poisons flow through the intravenous tube, the relationship can become toxic. And when little or nothing flows through the intravenous tube, the relationship can become anemic. To increase the amount of nutrients in a love relationship, it's helpful to understand communication skills, obstacles to communication, and conflict resolution.

Increasing Communication Skills

Because communication is both an art and a science, it requires a number of skills that can be developed and practiced throughout life. While this may sound obvious, it is not obvious to many people. Some people think that talking and communicating are synonymous and therefore they are no more skilled communicators in middle age than they were in adolescence or even in childhood.

It's important for couples to be familiar with the following principles of communication, to practice them, and to be able to make an early diagnosis when problems in communication occur.

Effective communication is simple. When sensitive issues are being discussed, it's helpful to reduce them to their simplest elements, then build on them as the discussion continues. In other words, the discussion begins with a topic sentence that summarizes the point or concern. For example, I say: "I'd like to talk to you about what you said to me on the phone this morning. You said that you think I use you sometimes."

In this example, no lengthy introduction distracts and creates frustration ("Why don't you just get to the point!"), no beating around the bush ("What are you driving at?"), no cross-examination ("What are all these questions about?"). The topic sentence is a plain and simple proposition expressed in an honest and matter-of-fact way.

Effective communication considers the time element. Timing is important in two ways. The first consideration is how much time elapses between the event to be discussed and the discussion itself. If the event is upsetting, a happy medium must be struck between attempting to communicate about it immediately—and thus risking that the attempt will be sabotaged by unbridled anger—and attempting to communicate about it so long after the event that the discussion will be detached and devoid of feelings. As a general rule, upsetting topics should be discussed as soon as the person feels that he or she can communicate with, rather than attack, the partner. In other words, there's such a thing as communicating too early and communicating too late.

Second, the topic should be discussed at a time that is reasonably good for your partner. For example, attempting to discuss tension-packed issues just before your partner leaves for work or right after he or she arrives home from work is likely to result in failure. Of course, for some people there is never a good time to discuss difficult issues, so they are always too busy or too tired. When this is the case, it is not simply a specific issue that needs to be discussed, but the quality of communication in the relationship.

Effective communication considers the location. Important or sensitive communication should occur in a place that is private and devoid of distraction and interruption. It is impossible to do justice to a serious topic when a partner is concerned about people overhearing the discussion, when the discussion is interrupted by people or phone calls, when the television set is on, when one or both partners are eating, driving, or working. Serious discussions should take place in an atmosphere where, for all practical purposes, the couple are the only two people in the world.

Effective communication is directed toward the right person. Sometimes when individuals are upset at a number of people, including themselves, they lump all their upset into one missile and aim it at their partner. For example, I'm 60 percent angry at my boss, 20 percent angry at myself for making it possible for my boss to criticize me, 10 percent angry at my mother, and 10 percent angry at you because you didn't remind me we had to go out to dinner this evening. However, because you're an easy scapegoat, I express 50 percent of my anger at you, a sum that includes proportionate amounts of anger at my boss, myself, and my mother. In other words, you give me one foot of stimulus for my anger, and I give you a five-foot reaction. Effective communication parcels out the anger appropriately, so that no one gets more than his or her share.

Effective communication is not self-contradictory. This means that partners should avoid sending more than one message to each other, in particular messages that cancel out each other. For example, a man tells his fiancée: "I wish you'd confront me more about my behavior that upsets you. That way I'll know exactly what it is and be able to work on it." However, when the woman accepts his invitation and confronts him, she is made to regret it. He says things like this: "*I'm* selfish! Just look at yourself! For the past month all we've done is what *you* wanted to do. Not once did we do what *I* wanted to do, and *you* call *me* selfish!"

More effective communication would have resulted if the man had separated the two issues: His feelings about his fiancée being selfish, and her feelings about his selfishness, and discussed them as two separate issues, preferably not at the same time.

Effective communication asks direct questions and receives direct answers. When questions are vague, confusing, or overly complex and answers fail to address the questions or are too indirect, effective communication can't take place. For example, a bad question is "Do you want to go out Friday night? I mean, if you don't, it's OK—maybe you're still mad at me, or you're too tired, or you just want to be by yourself, and all that's OK. I just need to know so I can block out the time. So, what do you think? Do you want to go out Friday night?"

A better question is "Would you like to go out Friday night?" A bad answer to this question is "Well, it's not a question of whether I *want* to go out Friday night. It's more a matter of *why* you want to go out with me. Do you want to go out so you can get drunk with your friends again and have me chauffeur you home? Do you want to go out and try to pressure me into doing sexual stuff with you again? Do you want to go out because all your friends are busy Friday night and you have nothing else to do? Or do you want to go out because you want *us* to enjoy an evening together?"

A better answer is: "No. Before we go out again, we need to have a long talk about some things that are bothering me about our relationship."

Effective communication is constructive. In a love relationship, even the most potentially upsetting messages can be communicated in a sensitive way. The motivation underlying the message differentiates constructive from destructive communication. Basically, there can be only two motives underlying communication: to be helpful or to be hurtful.

For example, I can say to you, "You know, I don't know if someone who just got two speeding tickets within the same week is in a position to call my brother irresponsible." This response is not an invitation to communicate but a challenge to fight. A more constructive response would be this: "When you criticize my brother, it confuses and hurts me. Let's talk about this, so that we can identify your concerns and deal with them so that this doesn't keep coming up in ways that are hurtful to me."

This response is honest, addresses the issues, and is an invitation to resolve them in a mutually beneficial way.

Effective communication means listening. For many people, communication means talking. For them, communication stops when they stop talking. In reality, listening to the other person is an important element of communication. And *listening* is different than *hearing* . Hearing is simply the physiological process by which sounds are transmitted to the brain. Listening includes hearing but adds an important ingredient: asking what the sounds (words) really mean.

For example, you tell me that you're going to have to cancel our date tonight because you're tired and want to go to bed early. If I'm only *hearing* you, I respond: "Actually, that'll work out fine. I can visit my folks tonight and get that out of the way for the weekend." If I am really *listening* to you, I would ask myself these questions:

Should I take her statement at face value? I'd like to, but she's been exhausted before and was happy to go out with me and have a good time.

Or is she upset with me or about something that does not concern me, or does she simply want to be alone? I need to invite her to discuss these issues so that if there is a problem, she can discuss it with me, if she wants to do so.

Obviously, a person cannot go through this process on every issue because it would only create tedium and tension. However, on issues that may have some direct bearing on the relationship, it's especially important to listen and not just hear.

Effective communication is forthright. Being forthright means being "up front," putting all the cards on the table. Assuming that the woman in the example above was not being forthright—that is, she had a hidden agenda—she should have been more honest. For example, she could have said one of the following:

"I got a letter from my father today that really upset me, and I know if we go out I'll be no fun. Then, you'll want to know why, and I'll have to discuss the letter with you, which I really don't want to do right now. It's better that I spend some time by myself, and we'll go out tomorrow night, and I'll be better company."

"Your attitude on the phone today upset me. I felt you were making fun of me, and I don't like that. I think you ought to give this some thought, and I'll give it some thought, and I'd like to discuss it with you tomorrow. If we do it tonight, it'll just ruin the evening for both of us."

This type of response would have been more helpful because her answer about being tired communicates smoke without pinpointing the fire. She's indicating that something is wrong, but by not clearly stating it, she is depriving both her partner and herself of the opportunity to rectify the situation; the fire may spread.

Of course, if people are in a relationship in which they figuratively get their hand slapped when they are honest, they will be forced into hiding their real thoughts, feelings, motives, and intentions. When this occurs, the couple needs to realize how destructive this is and take steps to rectify the situation.

Effective communication is balanced between positive and negative messages. Negative communications, such as messages that criticize your partner, can be accepted better when balanced by affirming messages. In other words, if it's appropriate to criticize your partner when he or she does something wrong, it's equally appropriate to affirm the partner when he or she does something good. Unfortunately, such a balance rarely occurs. People are far more likely to criticize their partners than to affirm them. It's as if people *expect* their partners to be perfect and only notice them when they make a mistake.

When negative–positive communication ratios are 1-to-1, the negative messages are likely to be better accepted. But, when the ratios run 2-to-1, 5-to-1, or 10-to-1, the communication circuits become overloaded with negative messages and fail to function adequately.

The Obstacle to Effective Communication

Effective communication among people of average intelligence has only one obstacle, and that is not wanting to communicate. Typically, people who experience problems communicating say they *want* to communicate, but in fact they want at least one other thing more than they want to communicate. For example, they may want to communicate, but they have a stronger desire to get their way on a particular issue. In other words, they are willing to sacrifice communication to get what they want.

Some of the main reasons that people don't want to communicate can be seen in the following attitudes:

I don't want to have to change, and if I really communicate with you, I might have to. Genuine communication requires *listening,* and I don't want to listen to you because you're going to tell me that sometimes I'm selfish, and deep down I know you're right. And, if I have to acknowledge you're right, I'll have to compromise with you on some of my needs, which I'm reluctant to do. Therefore, if I don't really listen to you, I don't have to change. I work on the principle that I'll listen to anything you have to say as long as it doesn't entail changing any of my favorite behaviors.

I'd rather use communication as a bargaining chip to get what I want than as a medium for sharing thoughts and feelings. I want more freedom to go out with my friends, and you want to talk about our finances. If you stop hassling me about my going out with my friends, I'll communicate with you about our finances. But, if you don't give me what *I* want, I'm not giving *you* what *you* want.

Not communicating with you is the best weapon I have to punish you for hurting me. For me to communicate with you means sharing some of my deeper thoughts and feelings, and you really feel very close to me when I do this. However, you hurt me yesterday, so I'm going to punish you by withholding myself from you today. When you properly apologize to me and promise you won't do it again, I'll begin communicating with you again.

I'm so angry at you I just want to hurt you—the last thing I want to do is communicate with you. I want you to feel as hurt and angry as I feel. I'm going to really tell you off and let you know what a jerk you are. After you apologize and I cool off, we can communicate, if you want to.

I'm right on this issue, and you're wrong; as far as I'm concerned, we can't communicate until you can see and admit it. Right now, I'm only interested in proving that I'm right, and you're wrong. After I've succeeded, we can talk about whatever you want.

I'm more interested in what's going on inside me right now than in what's going on between us. I'm distracted by my work right now, so don't bother me with any of your concerns because I'm just not interested in hearing them.

I'm not interested in communicating with you because you only want me to feel bad about what I said last night. You told me you were upset. I apologized for it. What else is there to talk about? Why keep going over the same thing? Let's just drop it.

These attitudes are communication-stoppers. The people who use them either make it clear they don't want to communicate or go through the motions of communicating while their real agenda keeps surfacing to sabotage the communication. Generally, it's better not to try to communicate on an issue than to *pretend* to communicate about it. It's more honest to say: "Let's attack each other for a while—let's hurt and make each other angry. Then, when we're through, let's sit down and really try to communicate about this."

Conflict Resolution

Every healthy relationship has conflict because each partner has needs, values, and perceptions that will at times clash with the other's. A relationship without conflict is dying or dead because the partners lack the energy, courage, or self-respect to assure that their legitimate needs, values, and principles are respected.

So the question isn't whether a marriage will have conflicts, but how many conflicts will occur, in what areas they will be, and how they will be handled. Resolving conflicts effectively requires both a healthy attitude toward conflict and the skills to handle conflicts in ways that strengthen the individual partners as well as their relationship.

Attitude toward Conflict

Many people have a negative attitude toward conflict. They feel that conflict hurts people, disturbs the peace, and can break up relationships, including marriage. This attitude is unfortunate because the person who has it is likely to avoid conflict as much as possible. The result is that the relationship is deprived of a healthy give-and-take to keep it in balance, and the couple is prevented from learning conflict-resolution skills, since there is little conflict. Consequently, when conflicts do arise, they are likely to be handled poorly.

Other people have a careless attitude toward conflict. They rush headlong into conflicts insensitively, running roughshod over anyone in their way. Their method of resolving conflict is to intimidate others into giving them what they want. However, this approach does great damage to a love relationship and ultimately can place it in serious jeopardy.

Still other people have a healthy attitude toward conflict. They understand that conflict, even periods of intense conflict, is normal over the course of a love relationship. They realize that conflict helps to clarify the needs, values, and perceptions of the couple as well as to temper the couple's behavior toward each other and to bring about justice in the relationship.

However, they also realize that conflict can be unhealthy when it is frequent, when it is handled destructively, or both. In other words, they view conflict in much the same way as they view fire. Fire can be used to cleanse and purify a material, but fire also can damage or destroy it if unchecked. These individuals neither avoid conflict nor instigate it. But, when it does arise, they see it as an opportunity to strengthen the relationship.

Two kinds of people must be especially vigilant when it comes to conflict. One is someone who was reared in a home with minimal conflict because conflict was viewed as bad and a sign of an unhappy, unloving family. These individuals are likely to view conflict as bad and go out of their way to avoid it, denying the importance of their own needs and values. Moreover, because they are not accustomed to conflict, they haven't developed good conflict-resolution skills, which gives them even more reason to avoid it.

The second type of person comes from a family with a steady diet of conflict, where if family members didn't battle over everything, they would end up with nothing. Conflict is so much a way of life with these people that they don't even realize that they unnecessarily are instigating conflict. In other words, they are fighting battles long after the war is over.

Conflict should be viewed as an opportunity to strengthen the love relationship. When conflict is avoided, this opportunity is missed. On the other hand, when the relationship is full of conflict, it will be weakened because each partner is either attacking or retreating much of the time, and neither strategy enhances trust, compassion, or reasoned discussion.

Healthy Conflict Resolution

The more couples increase their conflict-resolution skills, the less they will fear conflict and the more they will view it as something that can eventually enhance the relationship.

Couples who tend to handle conflict in growth-producing ways share the following qualities:

They precisely define the real areas of conflict and limit their discussion to one area of conflict at a time. This is in contrast to not being completely honest about real concerns or couching my concerns in terms of a secondary matter. For example, instead of admitting that I'm jealous that my fiancée spends so much time talking to her mother on the phone, I criticize her for spending so much time on the phone and then complaining to me about how little time she has for herself. As long as I'm unwilling to express my real concern, the problem can never be resolved. In addition, one sensitive topic should be discussed at a time, in contrast to "as long as we're clearing the air" discussions that include an entire litany of grievances over the past weeks or months. When this occurs, too many ideas and emotions are involved to handle any one conflict well.

Their emotions are under control. They can be very upset, but their upset doesn't override their reason and doesn't interfere with genuinely listening to each other. Sometimes a period of distraction and cooling off is necessary before a reasoned discussion can take place on a sensitive issue.

They *address* the *issue*, in contrast to *attacking* the *person*. Their focus is: "How can we resolve this issue?" in contrast to: "How can you be so stupid?" When people are under attack, they become defensive. Now, two issues are involved: the original conflict and the self-esteem of the person under attack. This will only further complicate and intensify the discussion.

Because they realize that conflicts are to be *resolved* and not *won*, they help each other clarify their concerns. This is in contrast to perceiving their partner as an enemy to be vanquished and certainly not helped. Their only goal is to resolve the conflict in the fairest way possible, and they know that mutual cooperation is the only way to go about this.

They understand that most conflicts are resolved through negotiation and compromise. Each partner will get something that he or she wants and fail to get something that he or she wants. This is in contrast to an all-or-nothing approach to conflict resolution which holds that to be successful one must win everything that is on the table. A "winner-takes-all" attitude will paralyze negotiations and breed resentment.

They understand that hurt and anger are normal parts of conflict resolution and cannot and should not be avoided. They understand that being hurt and being damaged aren't synonymous, that they can be terribly hurt about a situation but not suffer any significant long-term consequences. By the same principle, they can hurt their partner but not damage or destroy him or her. Therefore, they feel free to express their hurt, frustration, disappointment, and anger in constructive ways without fearing disastrous consequences.

Couples who handle conflict well also have learned to recognize caution signs that warn of potential trouble for a love relationship. Here are some of the warning signals:

If the relationship has a lot of conflict, with the couple going from one conflict to another, significant conscious or unconscious dissatisfactions probably exist within the relationship. These dissatisfactions should be specified and discussed.

If they are getting damaged as a result of conflicts (in contrast to simply hurt), this probably indicates some intense anger on the part of one or both partners. Damage occurs when one or both partners end up feeling very hurt, inadequate, or resentful and when these feelings last over a period of time and erode that person's self-confidence, as well as the security and joy of the relationship.

If conflicts seem to appear out of the blue, especially just prior to a time that could have been intimate, peaceful, and joyful, this probably indicates some significant fears of intimacy. Those fears should be addressed and worked through.

If the same conflicts keep surfacing in the same forms and intensities, either the couple does not wish to resolve them or a hidden agenda underlying the conflict needs to be addressed.

If one or both partners consciously or unconsciously enjoy waging conflicts as a way of creating a safe distance, wielding power, or venting anxiety or hostility in the relationship, conflict will be the theme of the relationship.

If conflicts are discussed with third parties for no other reason than to garner support or to be a tattletale, this partner may have more interest in winning a war than in resolving a conflict.

If one or both partners use negative strategies in conflict resolution, the conflicts won't be resolved, and there will be an abiding resentment. These are examples of negative strategies:

Blackmailing: "If you don't give me what I want now, I won't give you what you want later on."

Deflecting the focus: "*I'm* unreasonable! Let's talk about *your* unreasonableness for a minute!"

Ganging up: "Not only do I think I'm right and you're wrong, but my friends, my parents, and even *your* parents think I'm right."

Intimidating: "Sit down, shut up, and listen to what I have to say!"

Diagnosing: "If you really think that, you're either stupid or sick or *both!*"

Pouting: "If that's the way you are, I don't want to be around you."

Conflict resolution in marriage is a lifelong process that needs daily practice if couples are to handle conflicts well. If anything, conflicts will increase after marriage because the couple will be spending much more time together and the arrival of children creates its own set of conflicts. Therefore, it's important for couples to understand the nature of conflict resolution, to practice it regularly, to improve their skills, and to learn from their mistakes. When couples become reasonably good at conflict resolution, they look forward to conflict as a challenge rather than as something to dread.

Questions for Thought and Discussion

1. Assuming that no one is a perfect communicator, two areas of communication that I could improve are

   _____ and

   _____.

2. Two communication areas that my partner could improve are

   _____ and

   _____.

3. The best thing about our communication is

   _____.

4. The thing that needs the most work in our communication is

   _____.

5. My view of conflict in a love relationship is

_____.

6. My partner's view of conflict in a love relationship is

_____.

7. My typical way of handling conflict in our relationship is to

_____.

8. My partner's typical way of handling conflict in our relationship is to

_____.

9. One area of conflict that never seems to get resolved is

_____.

10. One area of conflict that I would be reluctant to bring up with my partner is

_____.

CHAPTER 7

Sexuality

Sexuality, an important part of courtship and marriage, includes not only genital sexuality but also psychosocial sexuality. A couple in love can act in many ways that are sexual—directly related to a male and female being in love—but never experience sexual relations. Couples who have had sexual relations before marriage will find that marital sexuality is often quite different from premarital sexuality and should find the information in this chapter as relevant to them as it is to couples who have remained celibate before marriage.

The chapter deals with two areas: a holistic understanding of sexual relations and some practical considerations about sexuality in courtship and marriage.

A Holistic Understanding

Sexual relations aren't a separate, independent dimension of the marital relationship. In fact, the quality of sexual relations is greatly influenced by an interaction of several factors that are intricately and often subtly related to each other. Sexual relations are not simply tacked on to the end of the day but, in fact, largely reflect the sum total of what occurred in the marital relationship during the current and previous days. Therefore, a holistic treatment of sexual relations in marriage includes an understanding of the personal and relational dimensions of the couple's marriage.

The Personal Dimension

The personal dimension of a psychosocially intimate relationship deals with what each partner does to increase (or decrease) the degree of intimacy in the relationship. This issue can be addressed by each partner asking himself or herself three questions.

The first question is: *What do I bring to intimacy?* The amount of psychosocial intimacy is the sum total of each partner's contribution. It's impossible to have one partner who is psychosocially intimate while the other is not. Therefore, to determine how much intimacy a partner brings to the relationship, the following questions can be asked.

Do I share my innermost thoughts, feelings, and experiences?

Am I honest about my feelings toward my partner?

Can I admit my mistakes and weaknesses in this relationship?

Can I be very trustworthy and trusting in this relationship?

Do I sacrifice my own needs when it is appropriate to give joy to my partner?

Do I create an environment in which my partner can be vulnerable with me?

When my partner shares sensitive information with me, do I affirm his or her efforts?

Do I give as much, if not more, than I receive in the relationship?

These considerations point out the difference between *having* sexual intercourse and *being* sexually intimate. Sexual intercourse is a physical act in which even animals can participate quite well. Sexual intimacy, on the other hand, is not just a physical act; it is part of the overall closeness of the relationship. It differentiates human beings from animals and selfish, uncommitted human beings from loving, committed ones. Therefore, a helpful question to ask in any sexual relationship, including marriage, is: Are we going to be sexually intimate tonight, or are we just going to have sex? Sexual intimacy is not something a couple performs—it's something a couple is.

The second question is: *What are my motives for having sexual intercourse?* There are some less desirable motives for having sexual intercourse, both within and before marriage. For instance, sex can be used as:

A tranquilizer, to feel good temporarily and block out the pain of reality. One problem is that a difference exists between sex that temporarily blocks out ordinary daily stresses and sex that acts as a painkiller, dulling pain that should be felt and used to make important changes in a person's life. Moreover, this motive reduces your partner to being a sedative.

A substitute for intimacy. In this dynamic, sex is used to feel superficially close to someone without taking the risks and doing the hard work that true intimacy requires. This motive does not allow the individual to experience the deeper joys of genuine intimacy. As a result, the person eventually finds sex with the same partner boring because nothing is involved in it beyond a fleeting physical pleasure. In addition, the partner is reduced to being a warm security blanket.

A means to an end. Sex can be used to hold onto a partner, to wield some control, or to manipulate a partner into doing what you want. The deal is this: I'll give you sex if you give me what I want. Sex thus becomes a business deal rather than one aspect of a loving relationship, and your partner is reduced to being a fellow entrepreneur.

A means of affirming your sexuality, attractiveness, and worth. Sex is used like a proving ground where a person accumulates bits and pieces of evidence that supposedly indicate that the person is at least OK, if not superior. The problem is that sex cannot prove anything, because so many motives for having sex are at work. In other words, the only reason a man may have sex with a woman is that he wants some sexual release, and he couldn't care less who she is or what qualities she possesses. This motive for sex reduces the partner to an audience response meter.

A weapon. Sex can be used to punish your partner. Sex that degrades, humiliates, exploits, coerces, seduces, or hurts is being used as an instrument of hostility, ridicule, and revenge. The problem is that the cause of the hostility is not being addressed and will continue as a serious problem. In addition, one's partner is reduced to being a punching bag.

It is rare for only one motive to underlie any act of sexual intercourse. More commonly, several motives, some positive and some negative, are present. Therefore, it is important to understand not only our motives for having sex, but also those of our partner. If, after sex, we feel that "something isn't quite right," we should examine the possible motives that sponsored the act.

The third question is: *What will be the effects of my having sexual relations?* Sexual relations don't occur in a vacuum; there are always effects that follow every act of sexual intercourse.

The desired result of sexual relations is that both partners will feel good about themselves and each other. However, one or both partners can feel good after sexual relations but for the wrong reasons. For example, maybe they used sex to make up after a relatively serious fight, but the factors that caused the fight were not addressed and remedied. These individuals should not feel good because they used sex as a bandage to cover wounds that will not be healed so quickly and pleasantly.

One or both partners can feel bad after having sexual relations because something bad just happened. One or both partners feel inadequate, unattractive, used, demeaned, or guilty. In this case, it's appropriate for both partners to feel bad. The hope is that they will discover why they feel bad, discuss it, and resolve it so that the same thing doesn't happen again.

Another result of sexual relations can be abortion or the birth of a baby. As obvious as this sounds, it apparently is not obvious to many couples. Each year in the United States, approximately 1.5 million abortions are performed, and this number has remained steady for the last decade. Moreover, about half the women who have abortions become pregnant, despite using some form of contraception.[1] Therefore, when a couple has sexual relations, they must be aware that pregnancy can occur. They must ask themselves what pregnancy will mean to them before the event takes place. To ignore this issue is to flirt with danger.

Another area where you and your future partner must be totally honest with each other is AIDS, a merciless killer whose victims in the United States increasingly are heterosexual men and women. Ask yourself, "Have I been involved in any activity, sexual or otherwise, that might put me at risk of contracting AIDS?" Ask your partner the same question. If either of you have even the slightest doubt, testing will be advisable if not mandatory. Remember, not only homosexuals and drug abusers contract AIDS these days. Many new cases involve heterosexual contacts, and you and your partner must carefully examine the risks of your prior sexual experiences.

The Relational Aspect

Because much has been written elsewhere about genital relating, this section will discuss the nongenital psychosexual dynamics of a love relationship that can profoundly affect the genital part of the relationship. Difficulties that occur at night in the bedroom are mostly symptomatic of problems that occur during the day in the living room or the kitchen.

Four psychosexual dimensions will be discussed: physical, cognitive, emotional and social. These can be diagramed in the following manner.

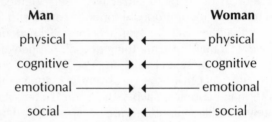

Man	**Woman**
physical ⟶ ⟵	physical
cognitive ⟶ ⟵	cognitive
emotional ⟶ ⟵	emotional
social ⟶ ⟵	social

The more these four dimensions are positive and mutually fulfilling, the more likely that sexual relations will be fulfilling, and vice versa. Courtship is the time to develop a real understanding and appreciation of these nongenital dimensions, so that sexual relations in marriage will be viewed holistically and not as a separate entity occurring in a vacuum. This section will deal with these four dimensions of psychosexual relating.

Physical. The physical (nongenital) dimension of a couple's relationship has four parts:

> How each partner views himself or herself physically. Do the partners feel comfortable with their bodies, or are they ashamed of or excessively modest about them? It is hoped that each partner is comfortable with his or her body. Tensions in sexual relations can arise when any other combination occurs, such as when one partner is comfortable and the other is ashamed.

> How they view each other physically. Do they view each other as attractive, potentially attractive, or unattractive?

If they view each other as attractive, no tension should be present in this area of sexual relations, nor should tension arise if physical attractiveness does not matter (which is rare, despite what should be the case and the couple's protestations to the contrary). However, if one partner views the other as potentially attractive ("She'd be attractive if she lost 20 pounds, which she's going to do before the wedding."), problems can arise when the potential is not fulfilled, or if it is fulfilled for only a brief time. Problems can also arise if one partner who believes that looks are important finds the other partner to be less than attractive.

How they relate to each other physically. Genital relations aside, people in love relate to each other physically. Some people are very physical; that is, they need a good deal of touching (embracing, holding hands, kissing, or other physical contact) to feel loved and to express their love. At the other extreme, some people feel uncomfortable with physical expressions of affection and prefer to keep them at a minimum. As long as the partners are fairly evenly matched in this area, they will experience little or no tension. However, if one partner loves physical expressions of affection while the other feels uncomfortable with them, tension is likely to result.

The strength of their sex drive. Each partner's sex drive can be strong, moderate, weak, or virtually nonexistent. No tension should arise in sexual relations if the couple is well matched—they both have strong or weak sex drives. Tension is likely if the levels are mismatched, if one has a strong sex drive while the other has a weak one. Although tension should not arise if both partners have weak or nonexistent sex drives, there is a question of how holistically fulfilling the marriage relationship will be.

Cognitive. The cognitive dimension has four parts.

How the partners perceive themselves. A partner can perceive himself or herself in a generally positive way, as attractive, intelligent, well-liked, competent, reasonable, mature, moral, kind, and strong. On the other hand, a partner can perceive himself or herself in generally negative terms—as unattractive, stupid, unpopular, incompetent, weak, or evil. These self-perceptions can significantly affect a relationship, including its sexual component. Positive perceptions communicate the message: "I'm a worthwhile person, and I'd like to share my gifts with you." Negative perceptions communicate: "I'm not such a worthwhile person, which causes me to hide parts of myself in our relationship and to suspect your motives for loving me."

How they perceive people of the other sex. Some individuals view people fairly objectively, regardless of their gender and may not generalize or harbor stereotypes. Others can have negative feelings toward the other sex. Men can view women as typically irrational, manipulating, moody, devious, emasculating, gossipy, and revengeful. Women can view men as typically insensitive, egotistical, childlike, spoiled, materialistic, power–hungry, and preoccupied with sex. When these stereotypes are present in one or both partners, they are likely to adversely affect the relationship, including the area of sexual relations.

How they share their private thoughts. The partners ideally are intellectually intimate, sharing thoughts (ideas, questions, confusions, dreams) that come from their deepest selves. Tension occurs when one partner is willing and able to be intellectually intimate, but the other is not. Tension is unlikely to arise if both partners prefer to share few of their private thoughts, but the question arises about how rewarding sexual relations can be between two people who don't know each other very well.

How they perceive sexual relations and how they probably will participate in them. Partners can perceive sex as attractive or repulsive, fun or work, a gift or a duty, spiritual or mundane, wholesome or depraved. And they most likely will participate in sexual relations in ways that are spontaneous or mechanical, joyful or solemn, creative or routine, giving or selfish, patient or hurried, affirming or demeaning, active or passive, voluntary or involuntary, intimate or distant, life-giving or life-depleting.

Ideally, a couple will match on all of the positive combinations. Tension will arise in sexual relations when one spouse views sex as fun and the other sees it as work, or one participates joyfully in sex while the other's attitude toward sex is solemn. Couples who match on several of the negative combinations may not experience tension but probably will underestimate and underuse one of the most precious gifts of a marital relationship.

Emotional.   The emotional dimension of psychosexual relating has four parts. The first part deals with how the couple share their feelings. Are they comfortable openly sharing their feelings of hurt, fear, anger, peace, guilt, joy, conflict, loneliness, affection, sadness, sexuality, boredom, and confusion? Or do they edit their feelings or prefer to communicate primarily on an intellectual level?

Couples whose abilities and needs to communicate on the emotional level match will experience little tension in this area. However, where there is mismatching, such as when one partner loves to share feelings and the other is uncomfortable with both sharing and receiving feelings, tension will arise and probably will adversely affect sexual relations. Couples who match in not sharing feelings will experience little tension, but they are also likely to experience little growth because emotions are an important fuel for psychosocial growth.

The second part of the emotional dimension deals with the kinds of feelings each partner has about himself or herself. People who generally feel good about themselves bring a positive aura to sexual relations. On the other hand, people who feel hurt, fear, anger, guilt, or confusion about themselves are likely to find true psychological and sexual intimacy to be difficult to attain.

The third part deals with each partner's feelings toward people and life in general. Partners who feel generally good about their families, friends, coworkers, school, or job are likely to carry these good feelings into their relationship, including its sexual dimension. Those who have some relatively intense and unresolved feelings of hurt, insecurity, anger, frustration, guilt, or sadness toward other people or situations are also likely to carry these feelings into the relationship, including its sexual aspects.

A fourth part deals with the feelings the partners have toward each other. No individual has purely positive feelings toward his or her partner. All couples, if they are honest, must admit that certain parts of each other cause them to feel insecure, hurt, angry, frustrated, or confused. The questions then become these: What behaviors in my partner cause me to experience these feelings? How deeply do I feel them? How do they affect the relationship? Have I discussed them openly with my partner?

If these feelings can be discussed in positive, constructive ways, they can strengthen the relationship in all areas, including the sexual area. However, if these feelings cannot be dealt with effectively, they are likely to fester and infect the whole relationship, including its sexual part.

Social.   The social dimension of a relationship has three aspects. The first part deals with the social life of each partner. Some partners get many needs met outside of the love relationship. They relate with family, friends, and coworkers in ways that are generally fulfilling and invigorating, and they are able to bring this energy into their love relationship. Other partners have minimal social lives and therefore bring very little new life into their love relationship, or they have conflict-filled social relationships that cause them to bring a negative energy into their relationship. In either case, the entire relationship is affected, including the sexual part.

The second part of the social dimension is the couple's social life within the relationship. Some couples interact well together. They do well when it comes to discussing things, disagreeing on issues, making decisions, working on projects, making plans, playing together, and confronting or encouraging each other. Other couples don't interact well together. A significant part of their relationship is spent arguing with, retreating from, or ignoring each other. In a sense, they *love* each other, but don't *like* each other.

Interaction within the relationship has a direct influence on how the couple relates sexually. For couples who interact well with each other, sexual relations are a direct reflection of the mutual fulfillment in the relationship. For those who interact poorly, sexual relations are a direct reflection of the mutual dissatisfaction, frustration, and emptiness in the relationship.

The third part of socialization deals with how well the couple socializes with other people, including their respective family and friends. If they socialize in mutually fulfilling ways with others, this can add a freshness and a vibrancy to the relationship that flows into their sexual relations. If their socializing is fraught with conflict, then it has a toxic influence on the relationship, and the toxins are likely to seep into their sexual relations.

If one spouse loves to socialize but the other doesn't, friction is likely to be present and adversely affect the whole relationship, including the sexual part. If neither spouse enjoys socializing with others, friction will not arise, but the relationship will lack an important source of nourishment.

Summary

Sexuality is a very important part of marriage. A serious mistake can be made, however, in viewing it as simply the act of sexual intercourse. Just as a ring is only as precious as the metal that goes into it, sexual intercourse is only as precious as the nongenital experiences that act as its setting.

Sexual Relations: Practical Considerations

Every married couple, regardless of how long they've been married, must deal with some practical issues about sexual relations. When these issues are understood and dealt with effectively, the way is cleared for a mutually fulfilling experience. However, when these issues are not addressed properly, they can interfere with mutual fulfillment. Four of these practical issues will be discussed so that when they arise, and even if they've already arisen, couples can come to a clearer understanding of them and handle them.

Attitudes and Sexual Relations

A person's attitudes toward sexual relations will have a large influence on how fulfilling these relations will be. Viewed positively, sex is:

A unique way to communicate deep feelings for which mere words are often inadequate. When you hear the words, "I love you," you *know* you're loved. But when you sense the embrace, touch and kiss of love, you *feel* loved.

A unique way of showing trust. It presents the opportunity to be very vulnerable. It represents one person opening up not only his or her body but also his or her soul to the other. It says: "I know you, and I want you to accept my being, and I know that you will not harm me."

A unique way of giving. When sharing your body represents sharing your soul, it epitomizes giving. It is a way of giving deep physical and emotional pleasure to another and enjoying the giving as much as the receiving. The giving is patient and unconditional. It is free and unencumbered with inappropriate expectations or jealousies.

A unique way of expressing gratitude. It is a profound way of communicating appreciation for your partner. It is one of the most precious gifts that a person can give to another.

Some negative attitudes toward sex that are likely to adversely affect mutual fulfillment are:

Sex is basically dirty and sinful and, while marriage can slightly rehabilitate sex, it doesn't rehabilitate it very much. Therefore, sex is a necessary evil in marriage and should be indulged in as little as possible.

Sex is a marital duty that is a part of the marriage contract; it should be rendered when a partner wishes to exercise his or her right. However, there is nothing that says sex must be enjoyable.

Sex is a lower-order behavior more befitting animals than intelligent, sophisticated human beings. Therefore, while one must participate in sex in marriage, it should be done as fastidiously and expeditiously as possible.

Negative attitudes toward sex are often caused by unconscious fears of sexuality: the fear of getting hurt physically, the fear that you will not be sexually adequate, the fear that you could get to like sex so much that you would lose control, and other fears. Instead of dismissing negative attitudes as ridiculous, it's more helpful to explore the possible fears underlying them and to address them with reason and compassion.

However, negative attitudes toward sex sometimes are the result of brainwashing early in life, and when this is the case, getting rid of them is difficult but not impossible. In either case, negative attitudes toward sex should be fully explored before marriage.

Timing and Sexual Relations

Some people can have sex at any time of the day or night. If two of these people are married to each other, they will have a good deal of compatibility, at least in this area. Other people, however, have a right time and a wrong time for having sex. If they are anxious, tired, depressed, or distracted, they are unable to get their minds, hearts, and bodies geared for sex. If they feel relaxed, loving, and sexual, they will be in the mood to have sex.

One type of person is not necessarily better than the other. But if one spouse is ready for sex at any time and the other must be in the mood, conflicts are likely to arise ("All you think about is sex—what's wrong with you?" and "You *never* think about sex; what's wrong with *you*?"). When this kind of interaction takes place, it simply compounds the problem.

In attempting to come to a successful resolution of the tensions caused by these differences in sexual readiness, it is helpful to keep the following points in mind.

Don't take these differences personally. ("How can you be thinking about sex at a time like this—you're certainly not very sensitive to *my* needs," and "How can you refuse to have sex with me—you must not love me as much as you say you do.").

Try to understand each other's feelings. For example, you may not be in the mood to have sex tonight, and your partner may not be in the mood to go on a family outing tomorrow. It cannot be said that one of these activities is inherently more important than the other. If we can understand our own ways of not being "in the mood," we may have a better understanding when our partner isn't "in the mood."

Sometimes when people aren't in the mood for sex or outings, only a little loving communication is needed to resolve the situation. Some genuine listening, patience, and compassion can do a good deal to help people relax, feel better about themselves and their partner, and gradually get "in the mood" when such a change would be helpful to the relationship.

Initiating Sexual Relations

Some people initiate sex easily, and if two of these people are married to each other, no conflicts will arise in this area. However, tension can arise in the following situations:

One partner almost always initiates sex, while the other partner almost never does. When this is the case, the partner who always initiates may feel confusion and resentment ("I feel that if I didn't initiate sex, we'd never have sex, and I don't know what this means: Does it mean I'm not attractive sexually? Why am I always in the position that I have to ask for sex?").

Neither partner is likely to initiate sex, yet each desires it. Each partner is afraid to appear "needy" or to take the risk of being rebuffed. When this is the case, frustration and resentment build and are likely to be displaced on other, less threatening issues ("Why do I always have to ask you to clean the bathroom after you've used it?").

One or both partners initiates sex in ways that have a chilling effect on the other partner. The sexual overtures are made in ways that are perceived to be crass, rough, or demeaning ("I was getting turned on until you started drinking and acting stupid.").

When tensions arise due to disharmony in the area of initiating sex, it can be helpful for both spouses to have an open, loving discussion of the issue. For example, one partner may initiate a discussion in this way:

I feel that I always have to initiate sex, which makes me feel needy and undesirable, and that I'm foisting myself on you. When you accede to my wish, I guess I'm supposed to feel grateful and indebted to you. If you refuse my wish, I feel humiliated and resentful. On the other hand, you tell me that you're reluctant to initiate sex because you were taught from an early age that sex is not nice, so when you do initiate sex you feel "not nice." You also tell me that when you do initiate sex, somehow you feel you have to make it worthwhile, and you don't feel very confident in that area. Then you end by reminding me that the last couple of times you did initiate sex, I was "too tired," which left you feeling undesirable and resentful.

With their "psychological cards" out on the table, the couple is in a much better position to empathize with each other and make some suggestions about what they can do to relieve the situation, if not completely solve it.

Unrealistic Expectations and Sexual Relations

Newly married couples often have unrealistic expectations about sexual relations, even if they were having sexual relations before getting married. The following are some common unrealistic expectations.

It is unrealistic for couples to expect deep psychosexual fulfillment every time that they have sexual relations, or even most of the time. To experience deep fulfillment, the couple would have to feel quite good about themselves, each other, their relationship, and life in general—not only at the same time but also at the time they have sexual relations.

In an imperfect world populated by imperfect people who have imperfect relationships, this holistic harmony is not likely to occur frequently, although it should occur more than occasionally. Most of the time, sexual relations run the gamut of being good but not great for both spouses, good for one spouse but not so good for the other, or not great but not horrible for one or both spouses, and sometimes they're horrible for both spouses, even those who are in generally good relationships.

Therefore, couples must walk the middle road between placing too much importance on sex and becoming alarmed if sexual relations aren't always fulfilling

("What's wrong with me, us, our relationship?") and placing too little importance on sex by dismissing generally
unsatisfying sex as immaterial ("What difference does sex
make as long as we love each other?").

It's unrealistic to expect deeply meaningful sexual
relations to occur without open, ongoing communication.

Some couples believe that because sex is a natural phenomenon, there is no need to discuss it. Other couples,
despite their protestations, are embarrassed to talk about
sex, especially sometimes with their spouse. In neither case
will the couples have much meaningful dialogue.

Open, ongoing communication is necessary for three
reasons. First, what feels pleasurable to one spouse may
not be pleasurable for his or her partner. For example, a
husband can't legitimately say: "I really enjoy oral sex, so
my wife will too." Second, it is impossible to generalize
about what will be pleasurable for a man or pleasurable for
a woman. For example, a wife can't legitimately say: "I
know what men like, so I know what my husband will
like." Third, something that feels pleasurable to a person at
one time may feel irritating to the same person at another
time. For example, a husband can't legitimately state: "My
wife loved it when I touched her breasts last week, so she's
sure to love it as much this week."

In a real sense, no one can become an expert in sexuality because the sexual terrain is always changing. Therefore, it's important for each spouse to keep an ongoing
dialogue with the other so that current information about
likes and dislikes can be shared and assimilated.

It's unrealistic to perceive the sexuality of a partner as
separate from the rest of his or her being. As was previously discussed, sexuality is intricately related to all the
other dimensions of personality (physical, intellectual,
emotional and social).

Some people ignore this reality and can create the following problems both for themselves and their spouse.
First, they believe they can ignore their partner or treat

him or her in demeaning ways during the day and have enthusiastic sex in the evening. In reality, however, this is unlikely to happen. More likely, the slighted spouse will approach sex with the conscious or unconscious attitude: "I'm going to get even with you tonight."

Second, they focus only on the physical dimension of their partner during sexual relations and not on his or her entire being. Sex for them resembles mutual masturbation much more than a sharing of warmth, tenderness, transparency, affection, and appreciation. When this is the case, the spouse who is the sex object feels used and denigrated.

Third, when sexual satisfaction is the sole focus of sexual relations, it is unlikely that much meaningful communication will occur after orgasm. What occurs between a couple after orgasm is often a good indication of their motive for having sex. If the purpose was simply sexual release, then the behavior after intercourse will be to move quickly to the next pleasure. To lie in each other's arms and share an intimate talk or a loving silence is regarded as a waste of time. If both spouses mostly wanted a sexual release, no tension will arise. But if one partner wants to have a sexual release and run, while the other partner wants to complete the act of love with loving thoughts, feelings, and communication, tensions are likely to arise.

Summary

If couples can understand that there is much more to mutually fulfilling sexual relations in marriage than simply "being good in bed," they will have a decent start in the direction of mutual fulfillment, which is a process that lasts throughout the marriage.

Notes

1. John Boykin, "Abortion: Which Life?" *Stanford Magazine* (December 1989): 31–37.

CHAPTER   8

Parenthood

For most people, the decision to become a parent is the most important one they will make in their lifetimes, and this includes the decision to marry. This is true for at least three reasons. First, a marriage is much easier to undo than parenthood. Parents cannot divorce their children or have their parenthood annulled. Once a couple has a child, they will be parents for the rest of their lives.

Second, parents have the awesome responsibility of forming an infant into a physically, psychologically, and socially healthy human being. Marriage presents no comparable responsibility. Husbands and wives are already formed and can take care of themselves.

Third, being a parent demands infinitely more time, energy, and continuous attention than marriage does. Although it is not recommended, spouses can go for days and weeks without directly paying attention to their marriage, and no significant harm will result. However, they can't drift along in their parenthood without destructive consequences. Parenting is a twenty-four-hour-a-day job, and there aren't many rest periods.

In light of the profound implications of becoming a parent, it is amazing how casually couples often approach parenthood. Many couples seem simply to drift into the decision ("Well, we've been married a year, so I guess it's about time to start a family."). Other couples base their decision on space and money considerations ("Now that Tom got a raise, we can move to a bigger place and start having children."). And still other couples, at least unconsciously, bend to peer and parental pressures ("Our parents aren't getting any younger, and they want to have grandchildren while they can still enjoy them.").

This chapter focuses on some basic issues that couples should consider while deciding whether to have a baby or when to have one.

The Welfare of the Individual Partner

The most relevant question about whether to become a parent is: How will becoming a parent affect my overall welfare?

At first, this may seem to be a selfish consideration, but in reality it is anything but selfish. If parenthood seriously impairs the overall well-being of a person, he or she will malfunction as an individual, spouse, and parent, and this can cause serious, far-reaching problems. In fact, it's selfish *not* to consider this dimension. When deciding to become a parent, too many people fail to consider their own welfare. They think only of the joy a baby will bring them, their spouse, and their parents, and they never consider whether they can psychologically afford to become parents.

The overall welfare of a spouse includes his or her physical, intellectual, and emotional dimensions.

The Physical Dimension

Do I have the energy to rear a child without unduly depleting myself? Some people seem to possess boundless energy. They can work all day, cook and clean all evening, and take good care of a house full of children. Other people, however, have very little energy, even during the least depleting periods of their lives. It takes a good deal of energy for them just to get up in the morning, much less get to work. By late afternoon, they are ready to collapse, and they vegetate in the evening and on weekends.

Even one child requires great amounts of energy. A child's needs are endless and require immediate attention, often at the least convenient times. As children grow older, their needs change, but the energy required to meet their needs remains the same or increases. A six-month-old infant demands great energy, but so does a six-year-old child and a sixteen-year-old adolescent.

When a parent's energy wanes and remains low, he or she will experience one basic symptom—lowered resistance to physical and psychological stress. The parent will be susceptible to such physical illnesses as colds and infections and vulnerable to such psychological symptoms as depression, impatience, sexual disinterest, loss of temper, and listlessness, among others.

These symptoms cause a vicious circle; they create problems that demand increasing amounts of energy to resolve. For example, if I don't have the energy to set and enforce limits for our child, the resulting behavioral problems will demand even more energy to solve. Therefore, one important question for prospective parents is: Do I (and does my partner) possess sufficient energy to do not only the work that a job and a marriage require, but also the work of a parent?

The Cognitive Dimension

Cognitively, the question is: Can I give a child the concentration that he or she needs and still pay sufficient attention to the other important people and areas in my life?

Children require a great deal of concentration. Parents must concentrate on what their children need at any given time, what they are really saying, what they are doing, where they are going, what is hurting them or making them happy, and what reactions to them would be helpful and unhelpful under each of a dozen sets of circumstances each day.

Some people have a wide range of concentration; they can fully attend to themselves, their work, spouse, children, parents and friends. Although they're not perfect, they do justice to each of these situations and relationships. Other people, however, have poor concentration. Either they can concentrate on only one thing at a time, or they spread their concentration so thinly over several areas that it's ineffectual.

People with poor concentration also create a vicious circle. Their lack of concentration causes them to make mistakes. They misplace things, forget information, misunderstand communications, misjudge situations, and daydream through important transactions. These mistakes create both personal and interpersonal tension, which further weakens their concentration.

People who lack the ability to concentrate do poorly as parents, and the negative effects often erode their marital relationship, leaving them feeling inadequate, frustrated, angry, and helpless. Therefore, an individual's capacity to concentrate should be taken into account when considering parenthood.

The Emotional Dimension

Here the question is: Can I share a wide range of emotions with a child without placing my emotional health in jeopardy?

Children need a wide range of emotional responses from their parents. They need to experience affection, hurt, compassion, anger, joy, fear, affirmation, loneliness, confusion, warmth, guilt, hope, and sorrow, among many other emotions. Healthy emotions push people toward good things and away from bad ones. They energize and give direction.

Some people can experience a wide range of emotions with others and feel energized. Others do not have a great many emotional resources. Transactions that include even the slightest experiences of being hurt or showing compassion drain them, hence the saying that someone is "emotionally drained" or "emotionally exhausted." When this is the case, work and a marriage relationship may tax the person's emotional resources severely, and the arrival of a child may seriously deplete them. The individual experiences chronic feelings of fatigue, frustration, or numbness, which he or she carries into all areas of life. This also creates a vicious circle in that the less emotionally responsive the individual becomes, the more frustration he or she creates and the more he or she reacts ineffectually to the emotional needs of others.

No one has unlimited emotional resources. Some people have just enough for themselves; others have only enough for themselves and their spouse; and still others have enough for a large family. It is important to determine where you fall in this spectrum when deciding whether to have one or more children.

Questions for Thought and Discussion

1. If I were to become a parent, I know that the things I would have to be careful about with respect to my own welfare are

   _____ .

2. If we were to have a child, the things that my partner would have to be careful about with respect to her (his) welfare are

   _____ .

The Welfare of the Couple

After considering the welfare of each spouse, it is important to consider how a child will affect the marital relationship.

It is often said that a child is a gift and brings the couple even closer than they were prior to the child's birth. This belief seems to be based on the idea that, in caring for a baby, the couple will work together closely, discover new and positive things about each other, and grow in the reciprocal love relationship between themselves and the child. In the past, this

belief was so strong that medical and mental-health professionals often encouraged couples who were experiencing marital
problems to have a baby as a way to hold the marriage together. However, experience indicates that such advice was
much more likely to result in even more marital problems as
well as parenting problems.

Today, both common observation and an abundance of research offer a different picture. One study was based on six
national surveys involving approximately fifteen hundred sub-
jects. Based on its findings and a review of the research on the
subject, the study's authors conclude the following: On the
average, children adversely affect the quality of marital relationships. This seems to be true with spouses of both sexes and
of all races, major religious preferences, educational levels, and
employment situations. Apparently, the "joys of parenthood"
did not compensate for the negative effects, which lasted even
after the children left home.[1]

Other research has generally found that the birth of the first
child often causes the most problems for married people,
sometimes reaching crisis proportions.[2]

In considering the results of the research in this area, it is
important to maintain a balanced perspective. On the one
hand, it would be inappropriate to dismiss twenty years of research on this topic as somehow flawed or unimportant simply
because it might make some uncomfortable. On the other
hand, it would be equally inappropriate to have a sense of
doom and despair with respect to having one or more children.

Two points should be kept in mind about these research
findings. First, the research renders *general* findings. Most married people found that children adversely affected their marriage. However,it doesn't indicate that *all* married people
found this to be true. Some marriages seem to flourish with
children, although this is not often the case.

Second, if couples can anticipate that the arrival of a child
will adversely affect their marriage, they can prepare for this
possibility and prevent or at least reduce its negative effects.

Some questions that can help in this effort are:

Whose idea is it to have a baby? Is it mostly the husband's, the wife's, or is it an equally shared desire? Spouses may not want a baby to the exact same degree. However, problems are likely to arise when one spouse clearly wants a baby while the other prefers not to have a child or to delay parenthood for some time. After the birth of a baby, reluctant parents can garner "proof" on a daily basis that having the baby was a bad idea, and this can seriously threaten the marriage.

Why do we want a baby? Any number of reasons may be present. So that we can be "a real family"? So that our marriage will become even stronger? So that we'll feel more complete? So that we can share our love with our baby? So that we can meet the expectations of our parents, society, or religion? So that we can perpetuate the family name? So that we won't become bored with each other and life? So that we can see a reflection of ourselves?

It is important not only to determine the principal motive for having a baby but also to examine the answers as honestly and realistically as possible. For example, the couple can ask: "*Exactly* how will having a baby bring us closer together?"

Whose baby is this going to be? Is it going to be mostly the wife's because she had the baby, and "women have a natural instinct for motherhood"? Is it going to be primarily the husband's, especially if it's a boy, because the husband can help the boy become "a real man"? Is it going to be the mother-in-law's baby because she's "already gone all through this and is the expert"? Or will both spouses share equally the joys and stresses of parenthood?

What is the cost–benefit ratio of having a baby? In other words, what are the specific benefits of having a baby, and how do they balance out the specific costs to us as individuals and as a couple?

What reservations does each of us have about having a baby? It is appropriate for people to have some reservations about any decision as important as the one to become a parent. What are these reservations, and how seriously should they be taken?

When would be the best time to have a baby?

How am I likely to react when attending to the baby preempts the time that we would ordinarily enjoy spending together as a couple? A thought to consider is the sentiment of some husbands: "I gained a child but lost a wife."

What agreements and practical arrangements can be made ahead of time to assure a certain amount of time together each day so that we don't lose the closeness we have?

How can we prevent the stresses of parenthood from interfering with our relationship? For example, what will happen when the baby wakes up every night crying? Will we argue over whose turn it is to get the baby or about whether to let the baby cry? Or will we anticipate certain stresses and decide on a fair and helpful way of handling them?

If having a baby means that one or both of us will have to spend more time and energy to do our work, how will this be negotiated, and how will the added time away from the family and the lost energy affect the marital and parenting relationships?

These kinds of questions have several layers of thought and feeling. Therefore, to ask and answer them at one sitting is to do an injustice to the decision-making process. These questions and answers require a good deal of honest thought and discussion and may well generate some tension. However, it's better to experience and deal with the tension in advance than to face it daily after the child is born.

Questions for Thought and Discussion

1. My most honest thoughts about having a baby are

   _____

   _____ .

2. On a scale of 1 to 10, I would fall at number

   _____ with respect
   to eventually wanting to have a baby.

3. On the same scale, my partner would probably fall around number

   _____ .

4. If we were to have a baby, my main reservation with respect to our marital relationship is

   _____ .

5. If I do become a parent, my primary motivation would be

   _____ .

The Welfare of the Child

Sometimes the last person to be considered in deciding whether to have a baby is the prospective child. It is assumed that any child would be happy to be born to any couple who wants to have a baby. However, both common observation and research indicate that a significant percentage of children have serious problems that often can be directly traced to their parents. Therefore, considering the welfare of the prospective child is an important part of the decision to become a parent.

Unfortunately, many perspective parents ask the wrong question. They ask: "Do I want to have a baby?" If the answer is "yes," they begin the process. However, this question has at least three difficulties. First, the question assumes that the people asking it know what it's like to be a parent. If, for example, they have had to do some serious "parenting" with brothers and sisters or were responsible for other people's children over a period of time, then they would have an inkling of what parenthood entails. However, if they've only casually taken care of brothers and sisters or other children for short periods of time, it's unlikely that they have a basis for deciding whether to have a baby. In this case, the couple needs to try to get some "hands–on" experience working with children and become familiar with some of the qualities it takes to be an effective parent.

Second, some couples want a baby simply to have *a baby*. They want a tiny, cuddly, frail, helpless, cute, and unconditionally "loving" human being to nurture, protect, and mold into their own image or perhaps into an even better image. However, babies remain babies for only two years, and then they grow into children and finally become adolescents. In other words, for eighteen out of the twenty years they are at home, children are not babies but are, it is hoped, growing into autonomous, assertive, and free human beings. As they grow, children need their parents less and less and often view parents as obstacles in the pursuit of their legitimate and illegitimate needs and values. When these parents "lose" their baby, they experience a sense of disappointment and anger that can last a lifetime. Or, they hasten to have another baby to replace the "lost" one.

Third, the question assumes that *wanting* a baby and *possessing the psychosocial competence to be an effective parent* are synonymous. The same people who make this assumption wouldn't make it in any other area of endeavor. For example, they would not say: "I'd love to be a concert violinist, so in nine months I'm going to be one." Yet, the skills required to be even a reasonably good parent are comparable to those needed to be a good musician. The real question is: "What psychosocial competencies do I now have that lead me to believe that I will be a reasonably effective parent?"

One way to evaluate whether potential parents have the proper skills is to look at the needs of children. Children of all ages need five basic things from their parents.

Individualized Attention

Parents both as individuals and as a couple need to regularly spend a fair amount of time with each of their children. Without individualized, private, one-to-one time between parents and children, no parent–child relationship can develop. There can be parent–child interactions, but no real relationship. Children need a close relationship with their parents to feel loved and worthwhile. When parents are attentive to their children, the children are likely to pay close attention to their parents, which is a basic necessity in the learning process. When one or both parents are too busy, distracted, exhausted, impatient, or bored to spend regular private time with their child, estrangement is likely to result, even in infancy.

Therefore, you can ask yourself: "How good am I at giving my full attention to people on a regular basis, even when it is difficult and not immediately rewarding? Do I do this well, or do I easily become bored and impatient and want to move on to things that are more interesting or gratifying? Could I give my full attention to my child after a hard day's work and after marital transactions that take a good deal of concentration and energy?"

Communicated Warmth

This means that each parent not only has warmth to give but also can communicate it verbally and nonverbally. Warmth means tenderness, compassion, peacefulness, affirmation, and sensitivity. Warmth is communicated by your eyes, tone of voice, facial expression, vocabulary, laughter, and touch.

Children need warmth from parents to feel safe, to feel good about themselves, and to feel an emotional bond between themselves and their parents. Warmth generally breeds warmth, while coldness generally breeds coldness.

Unfortunately, some people can communicate warmth to adults but not children. Others have warmth, but it's buried under so many layers of defenses that it rarely surfaces. And still others have little or no warmth, even though they may express love "in their own way."

The question is: "How warm a person am I, and how well can I regularly communicate it to others? Is warmth a part of my everyday response to others, or do I tend to be distant or businesslike with everyone? Could I share my warmth with a child who is frustrating me to no end?"

Graduated Freedom

This means that parents grant their children freedom in incremental steps from earliest childhood to adulthood. Freedom entails allowing children to make their own decisions to the extent that they are able. Children need freedom to grow in confidence, self-identity, and autonomy, all of which are necessary to live in the adult world. Unfortunately, some parents are overly protective or possessive of their children and usurp most of the children's decision-making powers. When this occurs, children become crippled, relying too much on others and lacking a sense of who they are or their potential in life.

The question here is: "How much freedom do I permit others? Do I let people, especially those closest to me, make their own decisions, even when I disagree with them? Or do I attempt to take over their lives, albeit in benevolent ways? Can I believe that even a two-year-old may know better than I what he or she needs in a particular situation, or do I think that's impossible?"

Healthy Discipline

This means that parents have the dedication and strength not only to set reasonable limits and sanctions on their children's behavior but also to enforce them consistently. Children need limits so that they learn what will and what won't work to make them happy and productive members of society.

Setting and enforcing limits teaches children self-discipline, self-respect, and respect for others. Parents who seem to be chronically tired, who don't like tension, or who don't want their children to become upset with them are likely to do poorly when it comes to discipline.

The question that can be asked is: "Do I set appropriate limits with myself and others, or do I tend to lack self-discipline? Do I avoid confronting others when their behavior impinges on my well-being?

Integrated Models

This means that parents behave with each other and with their child in ways that they want their child to behave. Children learn infinitely more from watching their parents than from listening to them. Parents who generally relate with themselves, their partners, their children, and people outside of the family in positive and effective ways are likely to provide a good growth map for their children. Parents who are unhappy with themselves, with their marriage, or with their life in general are likely to offer a growth map to their child that has many wrong directions and dead-end streets.

The question for the prospective parent is: "Am I well-adjusted, effective, and happy enough to be a good model to my child, or am I at a point in my life where I must honestly tell others, 'Do as I say, but don't do as I do.' "

Each of the above parental responses is necessary if children are to grow into reasonably well-adjusted adults. Parents who do well on four out of five of these qualities are still likely to experience problems. Ask yourself: Which quality of parenting could be left out with no ill effects on the child?

Questions for Thought and Discussion

1. Of the five things that children need to receive from their parents, I think I would do best in _____.

and be least effective in

_____ .

2. I think my partner would do the best in _____
   and would be least effective in

_____ .

3. With respect to becoming a reasonably good parent:
   a. I really think I could become one.
   b. I honestly don't know how good a parent I'd be.
   c. I don't think I'd do a very good job.

4. With respect to my partner:
   a. I think he (she) could be a reasonably good parent.
   b. I don't know how good a parent my partner would be.
   c. I honestly think he (she) may have some difficulties being a
      parent.

5. The thing I'd like best about having me as a parent is

_____ .

6. The thing I'd like least about having me as a parent is

_____ .

7. The thing I'd like best about having my partner as a parent is

_____ .

8. The thing I'd like least about having my partner as a parent is

_____ .

Summary

In summary, there are several points to consider:

Common denominators of all parental attributes are love
and sacrifice. Parents must be able to truly love their children and to sacrifice a great deal for them. People who
have difficulty demonstrating love and who know almost

nothing about pure (in contrast to tit-for-tat) sacrifice will probably experience problems in parenthood.

No one can know before becoming a parent what parenthood actually entails. But being *uncertain* and being *ignorant* aren't the same thing. It's possible, through a good deal of self-examination, reading, discussion with your partner, and hands-on experience with children to have at least some prior knowledge of what being a parent entails.

The timing of children is important. Just as someone may possess the skills to compete in the Olympics but not yet be ready to compete, a couple can have the skills to be good parents but not be financially or psychologically ready to have a child. Often couples need a few years of marriage to stabilize their careers and marriage before they undertake parenthood.

To plan before marriage to have a "houseful of kids" is likely to be ill-advised. Couples need to know how well they will handle marriage and then how well they will handle one child before they plan to have a large family.

In some cases, there will be disagreements between partners over whether to have children or when to have them. Sometimes these disagreements are simply power struggles ("You got your way on the last decision. You're *not* going to get your way on this one."). However, as often as not, these disagreements are based on legitimate concerns. To offer the most difficult scenario, it's possible that one partner is quite ready to be a parent and the other will never be ready, and both have good reasons for feeling the way they do. In such a case, the situation should be discussed well before the wedding. Furthermore, it is ill-advised for one partner to assume that the other automatically will increase his (her) readiness to become a parent after the wedding.

While there's probably a general relationship between the kind of parents a person had and that person's own parenting skills, the correlation is not absolute. People can have good parents and not be good parents themselves, while others can have inadequate parents yet be good parents themselves.

Similarly, a person could possess the skills to be a good partner but not a good parent, while another could have good parenting skills but not be an effective partner.

While a general relationship probably exists between being a good parent and having well-adjusted children, the relationship is not absolute. People can be good parents and have a maladjusted child, and parents can be ineffective yet have one or more well-adjusted children.

Parenthood is difficult enough for most couples, but for single parents it can be extremely difficult. It is for this reason that marriages need to be healthy and deeply rooted before a couple embarks upon parenthood (which is often a third career—work and marriage being the other two).

Research has clearly indicated that couples who decide to remain childless are no more likely to be selfish, immature, materialistic, or unhappy than those who choose to have children.[3] In other words, the motivation to have children can be just as selfish as that for *not* having them.

Parenthood, though difficult and even painful at times, can be a true joy. Some of these joys include a couple sharing their love and beauty with their child and watching the child clearly respond to it; introducing the world to the child and watching the child respond to it with awe and glee; and being looked up to as the most important people in a child's life—maybe even for a lifetime, and the feeling of joy and pride that accompanies this response. Other joys include being the primary teacher in a child's life, having the opportunity to educate a child according to your own principles and values, and feeling the sense of accomplishment that comes from seeing sons or daughters reach adulthood and watching them relate to themselves, others, and life in loving and effective ways.

Notes

1. Norval D. Glenn and Sara McLanahan, "Children and Marital Happiness: A Further Specification of the Relationship," *Journal of Marriage and Family* (February 1982): 63–72.

2. Barbara Thornes and Jean Collard, *Who Divorces* (London: Routledge and Kegan Paul, 1979), 89.

3. Linda Silka and Sara Kiesler, "Couples Who Choose to Remain Childless," *Family Planning Perspective* 9 (January–February 1977): 16–25.

CHAPTER 9

Cautions

The decision to marry is likely to be the most important one of your life, so it should be contemplated with a great deal of care. One of the truisms of marriage is that many marital problems were once premarital problems that were ignored or not taken seriously. Many divorced people can state accurately that the problems that led to their divorce were present in one form or another before marriage.

Unfortunately, people in love often put on blinders along with rose-colored glasses. The blinders block out threatening parts of reality, while the rose-colored glasses beautify the reality that can't be blocked out. As a result, many people marry a heavily edited version of their partner and only discover the unedited version after marriage.

This chapter deals with three areas of caution: trying to change behaviors that are unlikely to change, premarital abuse, and substance abuse in dating and courtship. The purpose of this chapter is to heighten awareness of these issues and to raise questions that should be asked before marriage.

Hoping Traits Will Change

Constitutional tendencies are rarely taken into consideration when preparing for marriage. This is unfortunate because these tendencies have a marked influence on our daily behavior and on the functioning of a relationship.

What are constitutional tendencies? They are potentials to act in certain ways that stem from a combination of genetic and intrauterine influences, meaning that they occur between conception and birth. (Therefore, to refer to these influences as "genetic" or "hereditary" may be incorrect or only partially correct.)

It is important to note that these influences are *potentials*. Whether they are activated and the degree to which they are activated will depend on how deeply the trait is rooted neurologically in the central or autonomic central nervous system (or both), and the ability of the environment to increase or decrease the trait.

The best thing that can happen to a positive trait such as healthy sensitivity is for it to be deeply rooted neurologically and to be strongly reinforced by the environment, with a family that values healthy sensitivity. The worst thing that can happen to a negative trait such as gross insensitivity is have it be deeply rooted neurologically and strongly reinforced by the environment, in a family that devalues sensitivity.

A question that can arise is: How do you know if a specific trait is constitutionally based or learned? There is no foolproof way of telling the difference; however, one can reasonably assume that a trait is constitutionally based if it was present since early childhood and did not change appreciably despite continuing opportunities to modify the behavior.

People who are courting must be careful about what behaviors they think (or hope) will change in their partner and in themselves after they're married. If a man says to himself and others: "Well, my fiancée is a little scatterbrained now, but once we're married and have a family that'll change," he may be making a serious mistake. A good axiom is that people should assume that neither they nor their partner will change much after marriage and make the decision whether to marry on that basis. People who think: "Well, I wouldn't want to live with him for the rest of my life the way he is now, but he'll change—he'll *have* to change!" may be in for a rude awakening.

The following are six constitutional tendencies that are particularly relevant to spouse selection and marriage.

Intelligence

Intelligence refers not only to an individual's general intelligence but also to specific areas of intelligence. For example, some people are constitutionally better than others in their ability to think abstractly, concretely, creatively, and logically; in their ability to perceive accurately, to remember, to reason well, to grasp the bigger picture.

This concept relates directly to relationships. For example, Merlin has the ability to think logically and is engaged to Martha, who has trouble in this area. While this discrepancy presents a moderate annoyance for both of them while they are dating, it can pose major problems after marriage because the stakes will be higher.

For example, Martha's deficiency in logic may lead her to make decisions such as: "I bought a new washer today because I figured as long as we're already in debt, a little more won't hurt." Her behavior is likely to create serious tension in the family. Assuming that Martha's deficiency in logic is constitutionally based and not acquired (for example, passive-aggressive) behavior, it is unlikely that she will change much in this area.

Sensitivity

People are born with varying degrees of sensitivity. Some are very sensitive, others are very insensitive, and most fall in the middle. For example, Theresa is reasonably sensitive to how she treats others. She is aware of their moods, vulnerabilities, what makes them happy and what hurts or threatens them, and she acts accordingly. She also has reasonable sensitivity to how others treat her—she clearly senses affirmation and enjoys it and senses rejection and doesn't enjoy that.

She's engaged to a man who is much less sensitive—a "bull in a china shop." Biff says and does the first thing that comes into his head without considering how his statements and actions will affect others. As a result, he typically says and does the wrong things at the wrong times in the wrong ways with the wrong people.

However, Theresa loves Biff dearly, so she makes excuses for him ("His father's the same way.") and thinks that her warmth and loving feedback will modify his insensitivity. However, not many people who know something about human behavior would invest much in her hope.

Resistance

People are born with various degrees of resistance to physical stress, psychological stress, or both. Tom seems to spend most of his life going from colds to headaches to stomachaches, all of which are true illnesses. His energy level is low, so he must pace himself carefully and avoid strenuous tasks to get through each day. Candice has great physical and psychological resistance to stress, so she is always full of energy and enthusiasm. She believes that Tom's aches and pains are "all in his head and as soon as he graduates from college and moves away from home, he'll be fine."

In fact, Tom will never be "fine" physically, and he may become more sickly as he faces the stresses of marriage and parenthood. As his infirmity increases, Candice will have less and less patience with him. After they're married, Tom will miss a few days of work each month or come home exhausted and be unable to help Candice with the housework and the children. A minor irritation to Candice now will become a major source of ongoing tension once she and Tom are married.

Temperament

Some people are constitutionally even-tempered, while others shift moods from happy to depressed for no discernible reasons. For example, Mary Beth is an even-tempered person engaged to Fred, who tends to feel "down" a good deal of the time. In this sense, they complement each other. It seems that only Mary Beth can cheer up Fred, which makes her feel important and makes Fred feel good.

Mary Beth believes that Fred's abiding discouragement, pessimism, and self-doubt are tied to his troubled upbringing and that her love and encouragement will help him blossom into a reasonably happy, energetic, and confident husband and father. However, if Fred's low-grade depression is constitutionally based, it is likely to increase under the stresses of marriage and parenthood and cause problems on many fronts: with work, communication, sexuality, and parenting.

Sociability

Some people are extroverted, others introverted, and most fall some place in between. Bob is an extrovert. He loves to be around people and enjoys parties, dances, and going out with friends. When he's alone he becomes bored and even somewhat depressed. Bob's engaged to Sandra, a shy person who is uncomfortable around people and enjoys being and doing things by herself. She likes to read, write, sew, listen to music, and spend quiet time with Bob.

Bob is very attracted to Sandra because she's "such a beautiful person." Sandra is attracted to Bob because he is handsome, bright, and "a very kind person." It bothers Bob that Sandra isn't more outgoing. He'd love to take her to parties, dances, and ball games and have her become a part of his group of friends. When she declines to go to parties with him, he misses her but also feels let down—as if she disapproves of his lifestyle or his friends. In addition, he feels guilty going out and leaving her alone. However, he puts up with it because he doesn't have much choice and because he hopes she'll outgrow her shyness.

While Sandra enjoys Bob's enthusiasm for life, she feels he's getting a little old to be playing softball and drinking with his friends on weekends. However, she knows that once they marry all that will change, so he might as well enjoy it now and get it all out of his system.

The problem is that neither Bob nor Sandra can or want to change. They're quite content with the way they are. The combination of their personalities is likely to cause tension after they're married and especially after they have children. Bob has two choices: to maintain at least a semblance of his social life, which will alienate Sandra, or he can acquiesce to Sandra's wishes and stay home, which will cause him to feel resentful. Sandra has the same choices. She can accede to Bob's wishes, go out with him and feel uncomfortable and resentful, or she can make Bob stay home with her and suffer his abiding resentment.

Sexuality

People differ in the intensity of their sex drive. Some people have strong sex drives, others have weak drives, and most people fall some place in the middle. Rod has a strong sex drive—just about everything he thinks about is connected in one way or another with sex. Priscilla has a low sex drive—sex pretty much doesn't exist for her except as an instrument for becoming a mother, which she very much wants to do. Rod always wants sex; Priscilla seldom wants it. The result is that Rod exerts sufficient pressure on Priscilla so that she participates in some sexual behavior reluctantly, which leaves Rod feeling frustrated and guilty and Priscilla feeling used and resentful. Rod's position is: How are he and Priscilla going to know if they're sexually compatible unless they experience more sexually? Priscilla's position is that if they really love each other, sex will fall naturally into place—after they're married.

Rod goes along with this, not because he agrees with Priscilla but because he has no choice. After the wedding, Rod can hardly wait for all the sexual pleasures he is about to experience. Priscilla is frightened because now she must face the fact that she is not very interested in sex, feels very uncomfortable about it, and would just as soon eliminate it from her life. Both Rod and Priscilla will gradually find that this is not a passing phase but a major impasse, and the problems that result could become great.

This example particularly lends itself to the question: Couldn't Bob and Priscilla work this out with some patience, tenderness, and love on both sides? The answer is: If their sexual tendencies are simply symptoms of immaturity then, yes, they can work together and come to a happy resolution of the problem. However, if their sex drive is constitutionally based, all the patience, tenderness, and love in the world are unlikely to bring about a significant change in either one of them.

Summary

It's important to avoid two misconceptions about behavior change. The first misconception is that all behavior can be changed for the better with maturity, a kick in the pants, or with patience, love, understanding, or counseling. This simply is not true. Many people in the midst of their broken marriages and sometimes broken lives lament: "I really tried to get him (her) to change, but it sure didn't happen; things only got worse."

The second misconception is that no behavior can be changed, and the appearance of change is illusory. In fact, much behavior, even constitutionally influenced behavior, can be changed to one degree or another, either in a positive or negative direction.

The issue in marriage preparation isn't so much whether behavior can change, but can negative behaviors be changed *enough before marriage* to demonstrate to all parties that the marriage is a reasonable risk? And, when behavior does change, will it change in a positive or negative direction? For example, a man's mild insensitivity may change, but it may change to profound insensitivity when he faces the stresses of marriage and parenthood.

Many dating and engaged couples put on blinders when it comes to negative traits in their partners. They either refuse to see them (even though everyone else can), rationalize away their importance, or expect them to disappear after marriage. The basic question is: If you and your partner would not change in any significant way in the future, would you want to live with each other for the next fifty years? If your response is: "I wouldn't want to marry my partner *the way he (she) is now,* but he'll (she'll) change," you need to answer the question: "On what do you base this hope?"

Questions for Thought and Discussion

1. What are one or two traits (whether or not they were discussed in this section) that my partner has that I really wish he (she) would change before we get married?

_____

2. What are one or two traits that my partner wishes me to change before we get married?

_____

3. What traits do *I* know *I* should change if our marriage is going to be successful?

_____

Premarital Abuse

Contrary to what many people believe, premarital abuse is far from rare. It cuts across educational, socioeconomic, and religious lines and can foreshadow marital and child abuse. Therefore, every couple should be familiar with this topic. If a relationship is free of abuse, the couple can learn the warning signs and nip potential problems in the bud.

Physical Abuse

In the research on abuse in dating and courtship, the following behaviors constitute physical violence: throwing objects at your partner, pushing, slapping, hitting with fists, squeezing, kicking, biting, hitting, threatening with or using a weapon. Studies on large numbers of college students found:

> Between 20 to 36 percent of dating couples experience violence in their relationship as perpetrators, victims, or both.

> In 65 to 70 percent of dating relationships where violence occurred, each partner had been both the perpetrator and the victim, indicating that the majority of violence is reciprocal. In short, violence breeds violence. Even when the violence always is directed at one partner, that person cannot be labeled the "victim"—he or she remains in an abusive situation. Therefore, it is often more accurate to speak in terms of "abusive relationships" than abusive individuals.

> Of partners living together, 83 percent experienced physical violence in their relationships, which is a higher percentage than either single people living alone or married people reported.

More than 70 percent of the violent behavior occurred after the relationship became more serious (47 percent during serious dating and 25 percent after engagement or living together). The evidence indicates that violence becomes more acceptable as the relationship becomes more intimate and is viewed as less of a reason to terminate the relationship.

When couples were asked to give the meaning of violence in their relationship, 73 percent reported it means "anger," 49 percent said it means "confusion," 29 percent said it means "love," and 8 percent said it means "hate." (Because couples could list more than one meaning, the above percentages total more than 100 percent.)

This is important information because it sheds some light on how violence can be tolerated in courtship. If violence simply means a partner is confused, then the couple may conclude that there's little cause for concern. If it is seen as a sign of love, violence can be viewed as proof of the depth of affection. This is in keeping with the finding that more than three-quarters of the couples in an abusive relationship did not think that violence had a negative effect on their relationship.

For most married couples, violence is not new. Forty percent of them report that violence occurred in their premarital relationship. As is true in the dating relationship, both the man and the woman can be perpetrators.

It has also been shown that 75 percent of spouses blame their partners for the violence. When they themselves use violence, they say that they felt they had no other choice and that any damage was accidental. Once again, it can be seen how violence can be tolerated in a relationship, including marriage. When partners feel they are not really responsible for their violent acts and that the damage from these acts is not intended, there's no real reason for them to change their behavior. As long as their partner causes them to react with violence, there will be violence.

The role of alcohol and drug abuse in violence has been researched and, while the results are inconclusive, it seems that substance abuse does not *cause* violence. A large majority of couples who reported violence in their marriage stated that alcohol and drugs were not a factor. And, when they are factors, it does not soften the problem but simply adds to it—the couple has not only a violence problem but also a substance abuse problem, both of which need to be dealt with seriously.[1]

Abusive couples tend to minimize the importance of violent behavior when they discuss it with others, stating that such episodes are isolated and that the relationship has improved markedly since the last episode. In this way of thinking, violence is viewed as almost a blessing in disguise.

Psychological Abuse

Psychological abuse is in many ways as important as physical abuse. In fact, physical abuse often (but not always) is a reaction to psychological abuse. The following are some common examples of psychological abuse:

Ridiculing a person, especially in sensitive areas. "If you keep gaining weight, people are going to think you're pregnant."

Making threats. "Wait until I tell your mother about what her darling boy did now."

Mimicking in hurtful, hostile ways. A man imitates the voice and mannerisms of his girlfriend when she's angry at him.

Withholding affection as an act of revenge. A woman withholds physical affection to punish her boyfriend.

Demeaning another's sense of worth. "If you act this stupid at your job interviews, no wonder you're not able to get a job."

Using past, sensitive information as a weapon. "I think you were right when you confided in me that you lost your last girlfriend because you were so insecure. You're going to lose this one, too, for the same reason."

Revealing confidential, sensitive information to others. "By the way, I told my mother that you thought she was trying to take over our lives, so that she can better understand your behavior toward her."

Embarrassing your partner in front of others. "Well, today was the day Jim was supposed to really confront his boss but as usual he backed down at the last minute."

Employing hostile vocabulary in sensitive communications. "Why do you think you're so frigid most of the time?"

Demeaning people and things that your partner is fond of. "I can't understand how you can call that slob who doesn't have a brain in his head your best friend."

Psychological abuse can also take the form of such nonverbal behavior as a facial expression (a sneer) or a tone of voice (sarcasm). Psychological abuse also can be omissions, such as forgetting important things or failing to give your partner some important information that he or she needs to avoid a bad situation.

Summary

The following thoughts should be kept in mind:

First, in a psychologically or physically abusive relationship, one partner is not the perpetrator and the other the victim. Both partners are perpetrators and both are victims as long as the abuse exists and the couple continues to live with each other. Abuse is a relationship problem that the couple must own and solve together.

Second, research indicates that when psychological or physical abuse is present in courtship, it often continues into the marriage and possibly even into the couple's parenting. Therefore, when a couple assures themselves that the abuse is simply the result of immaturity, drinking, fatigue, or stress and will not continue into marriage or parenthood, they are very likely fooling themselves.

Third, the biggest obstacle to resolving the problem of abuse in courtship and marriage is massive denial. Perpetrators typically deny that they psychologically or physically assaulted their partner, or they dilute the seriousness of their actions with protestations such as: "I didn't mean it." "I just lost my temper." "I hardly touched her." "He asked for it." "I did what any person would have done in the situation." "I had too much to drink, that's all." "I was just really stressed out." "It was all a big misunderstanding." "I just got fed up and finally put my foot down."

Victims participate in the same denial: "He didn't hit me—

he just sort of pushed me." "She threw a plate at me, but it was just funny." "He slapped me, but I have to admit I asked for it." "She screamed all kinds of terrible things at me, but she doesn't mean them and apologized later like she always does."

The subtitles to the explanations of both the perpetrator and the victim read: "It was nothing really, and it'll never happen again, so the best thing is to forget it and move on to another topic." As long as this attitude is present, the abuse can never be addressed and abated.

Fourth, promises and apologies play a major role in allowing abuse to continue. The promise, given with heartfelt sincerity, is that the abuse will absolutely never occur again. The apology, equally sincere and often accompanied by psychological or material presents, reduces the tension around the abuse and allows things to return to "normal," for which both the perpetrator and the victim are thankful.

However, under the weight of time and accumulated frustrations and pressures, the promises and apologies wear thin, creating the way for another bout of physical or psychological abuse.

Fifth, psychological abuse is not necessarily a lesser offense than physical abuse. An assault on the mind, heart, or spirit of a person can do as much acute and lasting damage as an assault on the body. There is never an excuse for hitting anyone physically *or* psychologically.

Questions for Thought and Discussion

1. In all honesty, do I see our relationship anywhere in this section, and if so, where?

_____

2. Everyone is abusive in some way or another in a relationship. What are the one or two ways I tend to be abusive and in what kinds of circumstances do they occur?

_____

3. What are one or two ways my partner tends to be abusive, and under what kinds of circumstances do they occur?

_____

4. How does each of us handle the situation when we are the victim of psychological or physical abuse?

_____

5. If abuse is occurring in the relationship, or would occur in the future, at what point would I seek outside consultation to get help with the situation?

_____

Substance Abuse

Substance abuse is epidemic in American society. A dangerous misconception is that substance abuse is a problem of single, inner-city people and not one of married, middle-class individuals. However, nothing could be further from the truth. Many married people abuse alcohol, drugs, or both, and often admit that the signs of abuse or potential abuse were present before the marriage. Therefore, it's important for couples to understand the nature of alcohol and drug abuse so that these problems won't "suddenly appear" after marriage.

Alcohol Abuse

The following are some thoughts about alcohol abuse that couples should be aware of during courtship and marriage.

Endless arguments can ensue between a couple about whether one or both has a drinking problem. While there is no way to prevent such arguments, it may be helpful to know the basic criteria that most experts use to describe individuals who have a drinking problem (whether or not they classify themselves as "only social drinkers").

They feel compelled to drink and to continue to drink until they become intoxicated. They *must* have a drink at lunch, or before, during or after dinner, at a party or a ball game. And, after they have the first drink, they *must* have a second and a third until they are intoxicated. Of course, these individuals don't think they are compelled to drink. In their view, they don't *have* to have a drink, or continue drinking; they just *want* to do so.

They refuse to limit or stop their drinking, either on a specific occasion or in life, although their drinking causes personal or interpersonal problems, including problems in a love relationship.

They feel they must drink to feel and function better. When they are sober, they tend to feel bored, morose, anxious, tired, irritable, listless, and insecure. But when they drink, they feel confident, energetic, alive, uninhibited, attractive and optimistic.

When they are drinking, their behavior typically changes in a negative direction in one or more ways. They become withdrawn, hostile, suspicious, boisterous, reckless, insensitive, abusive, depressed, forgetful, disoriented, imprudent, pugnacious, sexually promiscuous, or physically ill.

If one or more of these danger signs is present in an individual, he or she likely has a problem with drinking that may or may not have reached alcoholic proportions. It is important to realize that one need not meet all the criteria of alcoholism (for example, blackouts, withdrawal symptoms, absenteeism) to be an alcoholic or problem drinker.

Endless arguments also can ensue between a couple over whether one or both are intoxicated at any point in time ("I'm *not* drunk. Could I be drunk and drive this well?").

There is the misconception that unless people are falling-down drunk, they are sober. In fact, there are many degrees of intoxication between sobriety and an alcoholic coma. Some intoxicated people can appear quite sober to anyone who doesn't know them, just as dangerous electrical wiring can look fine to people who aren't electricians.

The problem is that one of the symptoms of being drunk is that the person thinks that he or she *isn't* drunk. Therefore, it can be helpful to realize what it takes for most people to become intoxicated. For example, when the vast majority of people have a blood alcohol content of .08, they are intoxicated and will manifest the signs of intoxication (problems with perception, balance, judgment, speech, thinking, emotional responsiveness). It takes less drinking than most people think to attain a .08 blood alcohol level. For example, a 150-pound person drinking a six pack of beer in three hours will have a blood alcohol level of about .08. Ordinarily, people who know a person well are in a much better position than the individual himself to judge whether the person has had too much to drink.

Problem drinkers often make the following protestations:

They don't drink excessively; they simply can hold more alcohol than others. Problem drinkers often can hold more alcohol than others because their excessive drinking has caused an increase in their tolerance for alcohol.

They never drink during the day. However, they may be "nocturnal alcoholics," intoxicated on many nights between 6 P.M. and bedtime, or "weekend alcoholics," intoxicated from Friday evening to Monday morning. In either case, the individual is at least a problem drinker and is doing a good deal of harm to himself (herself) and others.

They don't drink hard liquor, only beer, wine, or wine coolers. In fact, many alcoholics never touch hard liquor.

They are successful at work, have a good social life, never have been arrested for an alcohol-related offense, and receive no complaints except from the person confronting them with their drinking. In fact, a person can be an alcoholic and do well in certain areas. For example, great athletes and entertainers have admitted they were alcoholics, even during their most successful periods.

Denial and rationalization are two chief defense mechanisms used by problem drinkers. Denial means that problem drinkers either refuse to admit that they've been drinking or how much they've had to drink. Problem drinkers always have had "only two beers." Rationalization means that problem drinkers admit they've had a little too much to drink but have "good reason" for it. Something made them happy, so they're celebrating, or something made them sad, so they're drowning their sorrows.

Because these defenses are so strong, it is often difficult to have a productive discussion with a problem drinker about his or her drinking. Often, the only thing that has a chance of working is an ultimatum: "If you're going to continue to drink too much when we go out, I'm not going out with you anymore," or "Unless you modify your drinking or stop it completely, I'm going to break off this relationship." For ultimatums to work, however, they must be adhered to, or they will merely add to the problem.

Problem drinkers often have at least one enabler in their lives, and usually it's a fiancé or spouse. An enabler makes it possible, if not easy, for a person to abuse alcohol. This is usually done in one of two ways. One way is to view the problem drinker's intoxicated behavior as positive, at least at times. The enabler often enjoys the problem drinker more when he is drinking than when he is not. When he is drinking, he is more relaxed, loving, entertaining, cute, honest, sexual, and exciting. Therefore, the enabler either allows the excessive drinking to continue or, in fact, rewards it.

A second way that enablers can make drinking easy is to take care of the problem drinker and cover up for her or him. The enabler chauffeurs the problem drinker, lies to parents and friends about the drinking, covers up absenteeism with the drinker's boss, nurses the drinker when he or she is sick and hung over, and bails the drinker out of jail. Although these "acts of charity" are often accompanied by scoldings and threats, the problem drinker knows deep down that she or he has nothing to worry about—that the partner is enabling their drinking.

When an individual or a couple have problems with alcohol, whether or not they have progressed to being "alcoholics," professional intervention is often necessary. It's virtually impossible for one partner to help another resolve a problem with drinking. On the local level, most communities have hospitals that provide alcoholism diagnostic and treatment programs. In addition, Alcoholics Anonymous has local chapters across the country. On the national level, one can get helpful information from the following agencies:

National Clearinghouse for Alcohol and Drug Information
P.O. Box 2345
Rockville, MD 20852
(301) 468-2600
This is a government-sponsored agency that provides information on all aspects of alcohol and drug abuse.

Alcoholics Anonymous
P.O. Box 459
Grand Central Station
New York, New York 10163
(212) 686-1100
This is an international organization that has helped many people recover from alcoholism. Local chapters exist in many countries.

National Council on Alcoholism
12 West 21st Street
New York, New York 10010
(212) 206-6770
The Council works for the prevention and control of alcoholism by providing information on the problem.

In summary, because alcohol is both a chemical and a psychological addiction, it must be treated by professionals who specialize in the diagnosis and treatment of the serious medical, psychological, and spiritual ramifications that alcoholism presents.

Drug Abuse

The concept of drug abuse covers two kinds of situations: illegal drugs and the abuse of prescription drugs.

Illegal drugs include cocaine, crack cocaine, marijuana and hashish, heroin, and hallucinogens (LSD, PCP, mescaline, and peyote).

Three basic problems exist with using illegal drugs. First, they can be highly addicting physically or psychologically, or both, and can take over or seriously interfere with the user's life.

Second, because these drugs are illegal, users often must associate with unsavory people to get drugs, and they risk getting arrested—a risk that is increasing as law enforcement agencies crack down on "casual users." An arrest record in many cases will follow the user for the rest of his or her life.

Third, users of illegal drugs typically ask their friends to give them money for drugs or try to get their friends to use drugs with them. It is not uncommon that, when one partner in a relationship uses drugs, sooner or later the other one will also.

When illegal drug use is practiced by a couple who plans to marry, they should ask themselves and each other the following questions:

What is lacking in life that one or both of us need to use illegal drugs to feel good? If the answer is "Nothing," then the question arises: Then why use them when the risks on all sides are so great?

How does the use of illegal drugs, even if it's only occasional, affect the love relationship? If use has no effect, why is it that both partners are concerned about the use of illegal drugs? If there is an effect, what is it, and what should be done in the face of that effect?

Do we think that the abuse will stop after the wedding day? If so, on what evidence is this hope or expectation based? If not, how does illegal drug use fit in with the couple's idea of a happy and healthy family?

A second problem with drugs is the abuse of legal, prescription drugs. There are three main categories of psychoactive drugs that affect the intellect and emotions: sedatives (barbiturates, tranquilizers), narcotics, and stimulants (amphetamines).

People take sedatives to feel less stressed, to reduce their blood pressure, and to sleep better. Some common sedatives are: Nembutal, Amytal, Seconal, Valium, and Dalmane.

People take narcotics to alleviate pain and to feel peaceful and euphoric. Common narcotics or analgesics—drugs that reduce pain—include morphine, codeine, Demerol, Darvon, and methadone.

People take stimulants to increase energy, remain alert, enhance self-confidence, fight depression, and lose weight. Some common stimulants are Benzedrine, Dexedrine, Ritalin Hydrochloride, Tenuate, Preludin, and Methedrine.

Tolerance increases rapidly for all these drugs, meaning that higher dosages are required to attain the same effect. In addition, physical or psychological addiction is common with these drugs, even after only short periods of use.

If one or both partners are using prescribed psychoactive drugs, the couple should ask themselves these questions:

Why is the drug being taken? If the person is so depressed that he must take medication, what is causing this depression? If he or she is under so much stress that medication is necessary, what is causing the stress? If the person doesn't have enough confidence or energy to face the day, what's the problem?

The answers to these questions are very important because a person can't take these psychoactive drugs forever without becoming addicted and doing great damage to himself (herself) and others. Sooner or later, the individual must face the psychosocial factors that are causing or contributing to the problem and deal directly with them, making it possible to discontinue the drug.

Often, people continue to take psychoactive drugs because

they are addicted to them and not because they are "depressed" or "want to lose weight."

Is taking the drug absolutely necessary? Were all other avenues tried before beginning and continuing the drug? Did the individual attempt to make the necessary changes in his or her life before taking the medication? Did she seek the help of family, friends, or a professional counselor to deal with the causes of anxiety, depression, or lack of confidence? Or are the medications viewed as an easy, magical cure for all problems?

How long does the person plan to take the medication? Does he (she) plan to take it forever? Does he plan to discontinue it before the wedding? If so, why does he think he'll be able to function without it then when he feels he can't do so now?

How might taking the medications be adversely affecting the person, the love relationship or both?

Is the person taking the medication in appropriate ways? Is she (he) taking the proper dosage at the proper time? Is she being closely monitored by the prescribing physician for adverse biochemical and behavioral changes due to the medication? Is she working with one physician, or is she getting prescriptions from more than one doctor?

Summary

Both alcohol abuse and drug (legal and illegal) abuse cause monumental problems in marriage. Many marriage complaints that couples bring to counselors and therapists are caused or complicated by substance abuse, even when the couple may see no connection between their problem and the substance abuse. For this reason, it is important to make an honest evaluation of the situation before marriage and to monitor it throughout marriage. Issues, questions, and problems that can be faced and dealt with before marriage prevent a good deal of unnecessary anguish after marriage and parenthood.

Questions for Thought and Discussion

1. Does my partner have even the slightest reason to be concerned about me with regard to substance abuse?

_____

2. Do I have even the slightest reason to be concerned about my partner with regard to substance abuse?

_____

3. As a couple, what danger signs should we be aware of with respect to substance use, and at what point would we consider getting professional help?

_____

Notes

1. Information contained in this section is based on the following sources: Rodney Cate, June M. Henton, James Koval, F. Scott Christopher, and Sally Lloyd, "Premarital Abuse: A Social Psychological Perspective," *Journal of Family Issues* (March 1982): 79–90. June Henton, Rodney Cate, James Koval, Sally Lloyd, and F. Scott Christopher, "Romance and Violence in Dating Relationships," *Journal of Family Issues* (September 1983): 467–82; Katherine E. Lane and Patricia A. Gwartney-Gibbs, "Violence in the Context of Dating and Sex," *Journal of Family Issues* (March 1985): 45–59.

CHAPTER 10

Problems

Every marriage has problems, and most marriages have serious problems at one point or another. To expect anything else is unrealistic. Having marital problems is difficult enough, but most problems become compounded when a couple thinks that they shouldn't have them. For example, a couple may encounter a problem of boredom in their marriage but, because they think this indicates something is seriously wrong with them or their marriage, they have a twofold problem. Therefore, it's important for couples to recognize some of the problems they are likely to encounter in marriage so they can place the problems in a proper perspective and get a head start on handling them.

Boredom

Courtship is rarely boring. Each date offers new discoveries. Some of the discoveries are exciting and others are depressing, but they are not boring. In addition, the dating couple has parties to attend, projects to do together, dances, camping trips, vacations, loving talks, lively arguments. And, if things do get boring in the relationship, each partner can visit friends, family, or simply read a good book. The concepts of boredom and courtship seldom appear together.

However, things change for most couples after marriage, either gradually or immediately, especially after the first child arrives. Most of the previously unexplored parts of each individual have been discovered, and new discoveries are more likely to be negative than positive ("I always knew you were sloppy, but not *this* sloppy!"). The wife has heard her husband's stories many times and is tired of them, especially when she has work to be done. The husband who found sexual relations with his wife so exhilarating in the earlier stages of the marriage now sometimes falls asleep and snores in the midst of them.

Furthermore, socializing with friends becomes more difficult as time, energy, and finances become less abundant. As the routines of marriage and parenthood set in, boredom begins to occur. And, if couples aren't careful, they can begin to blame each other, or the institutions of marriage and parenthood, or themselves for this boredom, which is a source of stress in a marriage.

However, couples can be aware of five points about boredom. First, boredom is normal. While some couples never seem to experience boredom, most do. Unless boredom becomes a theme of the marriage, it should not be viewed as a cancer any more than occasional arguments are.

Second, occasional boredom never hurt any person or relationship, so you don't need to feel you must jump up and do something about it. Couples can experience a boring weekend once in a while and remain unscathed.

Third, you don't have to suffer boredom in silence. There's nothing wrong with saying, "I'm bored—let's go to a movie tonight (or go on a picnic, or go for a ride, or visit friends)." Marriage will be boring at times, but it's not *mandatory* that marriage remain boring.

Fourth, one of the most hurtful things that one partner can

directly or indirectly communicate to the other is that he or she is boring. To accuse your partner of being boring is to do a damaging thing, something that will instantly cure the problem of boredom, but at great expense to the relationship.

Finally, if boredom is more than occasional, some dysfunction is likely to exist in the relationship. Frequently, the problem for a couple who once found each other interesting is that they've become scared of each other, angry at each other, or both. They're scared because they tried to be honest and paid a high price for it, so they've decided to keep their feelings to themselves. Or they're angry and are withholding themselves from each other. The result is that only the most superficial and practical issues are discussed, thus creating boredom. When this is the case, one or both partners are likely to complain that the other partner is boring, or that marriage is boring. They will become depressed or look elsewhere for some excitement. If a partner finds excitement elsewhere, he or she will be less inclined to work at the cause of boredom in the marriage, which will perpetuate the problem. If the partner is unsuccessful in finding excitement elsewhere, he or she is likely to become increasingly stressed or depressed as the boredom increases.

Boredom is to be expected in marriage, and couples who are prepared for it are likely to deal with it constructively.

Questions for Thought and Discussion

1. What bores me the most in life, and can I expect any of these things to be a normal part of marriage and parenthood?

_____

2. When I am bored, what do I usually do? Endure it? Blame others for it? Do something constructive about it? Stir up trouble?

_____

3. How will my partner handle the inevitably boring parts of marriage and parenthood?

Feeling Used

If partners didn't feel they were being used before marriage, they are likely to feel so after marriage and the arrival of children. One reason is that the partners *are* being used. Even in the best relationships, including marriage, two kinds of motives exist: self-centered and altruistic. If the two are in balance, the relationship should be quite good. And, when this is the case, 50 percent of a day's interactions are based on self-centered motives, which effectively say: "Here's what you can do to make me happy right now." Even in the best marriages, therefore, one partner may be using the other for his or her fulfillment half of the time. Consequently, it's appropriate for each partner to feel used in marriage.

A partner also can feel used if he or she uses selective perception. For example: "I feel used when you ask me to drive your mother to her physiotherapist's office every Wednesday. After all, she is *your* mother, she does have friends who can drive her, and I have my own chores to do." That's one perception. Here is a more balanced one. "When I think about it, I see that you work an extra ten hours a week so that we can afford the down payment on a home in an area that will be close to my parents. When we compare the amount of time and energy you spend each week to help me get my wish with the hours I spend helping your mother, I see a different picture." The point is that we tend to be quite sensitive to people using us but are far less sensitive to the fact that we also use other people.

A third reason that partners feel used can be traced to semantics. They confuse using someone and asking someone to cooperate. Usually, people feel this way: "I ask you to *cooperate* with me, but you *use* me." For example, I can ask you to cooperate with me and drive my mother to the doctor without *using* you. Marriage requires a tremendous amount of cooperation—of give and take. To look at the "give" part as being used is to misunderstand one of the basic elements of marriage and parenthood, namely, cooperation.

Finally, partners can feel used not only because they are being used (which is normal and a necessary part of marriage), but also because they are being *abused*. Abused means that one partner's ratio between self-centered and altruistic impulses is 50-to-50, while the other's is 90-to-10. In other words, in the give and take of marriage, the second partner is giving 10 percent of the time and taking 90% of the time. In this case, significant problems are likely to arise and will continue to plague the relationship until the give-and-take ratios become more equal.

It should be noted that give-and-take ratios don't just deal with quantity (how much each partner gives) but quality (what each partner gives). For example, a successful businessman may give his wife a few expensive gifts each year and feel this covers his debts to her. In reality, his wife may need her husband to provide not gifts but a lot more time, attention, affection, and help with the children, which the husband is unable or unwilling to give. Therefore, while the husband views himself as more than generous to his wife, she sees him as very stingy in the areas that really matter to her. In other words, the husband gives his wife what *he* wants—not what *she* wants.

So, being used is a normal and necessary part of marriage. It is to be expected, but it also is to be differentiated from abuse, which is a destructive force in marriage.

Questions for Thought and Discussion

1. Once in a while I feel used in our relationship when the following things occur

_____

_____ .

2. I have to admit that, like everyone else, I use people sometimes. The ways I use my partner and don't always feel good
about it are

_____

_____ .

3. Once in a while, I think my partner uses me in ways I don't
feel completely comfortable with. Examples of this are

_____

_____ .

Suffering

Suffering is another concept that is rarely mentioned in the
same breath as marriage and parenthood. In fact, it's likely that
one of the unconscious reasons for marrying is to escape the
suffering people envision would come to them if they were to
remain single—loneliness, no children, no one to care for them
in their old age, no meaningful purpose in life.

The truth is, however, that both marriage and parenthood
have their share of suffering. Therefore, it's important to understand something about the nature of suffering. The concept of
suffering, at least as it's used here, refers to intense psychological pain of short or long duration. Suffering does not include
the daily minor hurts that are a part of marriage and parenthood, but only those that are significant.

A basic cause of suffering is the realization, which may be
gradual or sudden, that a priority need in marriage and parenthood is not going to get met, or has stopped getting met.

Suffering in Marriage

Some realizations, which may be gradual or sudden and can
cause significant suffering in marriage are:

A wife learns that she will never be as exciting or fulfilling for her husband as his career is.

A husband learns that, once the first child arrives, he will never again be the primary focus of his wife's affection.

A wife learns that her body is often more attractive to her husband than is her soul.

A husband learns that his wife's respect for him is highly dependent on how successful he is both materially and professionally.

A wife learns that her husband has seldom found her to be intellectually interesting.

A husband learns that his wife has a habit of criticizing him behind his back to their children, friends, and relatives.

A wife learns that her husband really doesn't love her as much as she loves him.

A husband learns that his wife has rarely enjoyed having sex with him.

A wife learns that her husband has a serious drinking problem.

A husband learns that his wife has always wished he was a more confident, strong, and influential person.

A wife learns her husband always wished that she was more sexually alluring and active.

A husband learns that his wife has been unfaithful to him.

A wife learns her husband doesn't want her to have a life of her own.

A husband learns that his wife has been dishonest with him over such matters as how much money she spends on things for herself and friends.

A wife learns that her husband has little intention of including her in any major decisions, especially those that involve finances.

Any of these realizations can cause suffering in most people. Their intensity depends on each person's psychological makeup, the overall strength of the marriage, and how the suffering is handled.

Suffering in Parenthood

Parenthood also involves some suffering. Here are some examples:

A child, for whatever reasons, rejects the affection of one or both parents. This can occur in early infancy, or in childhood, adolescence, or adulthood. No matter how much the parents genuinely love the child, and no matter how much they demonstrate their love, sometimes at great sacrifice, it runs off the child's psyche, like water off a duck's back.

A child may have a personality that one or both parents finds abrasive ("He's sure not like any of us."). The more they try to mold the child's personality into "the family's personality," the more stubborn and obnoxious the child becomes. Over time, the parents and the child come to deeply dislike each other, although the parents would never admit it.

A child may be impaired, either genuinely impaired physically or psychologically, or impaired only in light of the parents' unrealistic standards. For example, while the child is average, the parents don't want an average child. Their dreams and sacrifices are based on a child who will be superior physically, intellectually, socially, artistically, or in all ways. The significant discrepancy between their dreams and reality causes them and their child a good deal of suffering.

A son or daughter, for whatever reasons, does not come close to realizing his or her potential, preferring to take the path of least resistance.

A son or daughter may have a problem with discipline and often be in conflict with parents, teachers, neighbors, and law enforcement agencies. This causes the parents anguish, embarrassment, and financial loss.

A son or daughter may become addicted to alcohol, drugs, or both, become psychosocially impaired, and commit crimes often related to addiction (burglary, rape, armed robbery, impaired driving, assaults, among others).

A son or daughter rebels against the parents and demonstrates this by running away from home, getting pregnant, entering into an improbable marriage, attacking the parents or ostracizing them.

A son or daughter receives all the psychological and material support parents can offer but treats them in ungrateful and disrespectful ways, never demonstrating gratitude, affection, or loyalty.

It would be rare for marriage and parenthood not to include a significant amount of suffering. However, it is important to keep in mind a few points about the nature of suffering. First, suffering need not be destructive to you or to marital or parental relationships. Common observation indicates that many people suffer a great deal and, rather than being destroyed, become stronger as a result of the suffering. This is true not only of individuals but of relationships and institutions. Like an arm or a leg, a marriage or parenting relationship can become fractured but not destroyed. With proper diagnosis, treatment, and healing, the person and the relationship can become stronger than ever. This is true even in such cases of acute trauma and suffering as substance or spousal abuse, incest, infidelity, arrest, or scandal.

Second, because this is so, it is not helpful for future

spouses to set certain "catastrophic escape clauses" for remaining in or leaving their marriage. For example, the person who says: "I'll put up with anything in my marriage except infidelity," may be painting himself or herself into a destructive corner. Infidelity is often a symptom of a marital problem for which both partners share some responsibility and, if the problem can be correctly diagnosed and treated, the marriage may become stronger than it ever was. An automatic divorce as a response to infidelity may be precipitous, unnecessary, and do much more harm than good to all concerned.

Finally, it is important to distinguish between suffering that damages but does not destroy and suffering that both damages *and* destroys. The institutions of marriage and parenthood were never meant to destroy people. If, despite all attempts to remedy the situation, spouses or children are genuinely being destroyed, then whether to continue the life of the family as a unit must be seriously questioned.

Injustice

Marriage contains a lot of real and imagined injustice. It's not unusual for spouses to complain silently to themselves or loudly to each other: "You're not being fair about this!" Injustice occurs in marriage (and most close relationships) because sometimes spouses have conflicting needs and only one set can be met at a time. All human beings, including those who love each other, have a selfish streak that causes them to want their way over anyone else's.

The following are some areas in which injustice can occur:

Money

Money can be a source of conflict for many reasons. One of the biggest problems involves fairness. For example, a husband works hard for the money he makes, and his wife doesn't work or brings home an income much less than his. He believes that he should have the majority vote in how the money is spent because he makes most or all of it and knows more about financial matters than his wife.

His wife finds this unfair because she feels the money is family money, not just her husband's, and she has as much right to say how the money should be spent as he does. Moreover, she doesn't think his justifications for making the decisions are good ones. On the other hand, she makes the majority of the decisions regarding the children, including very important ones dealing with schooling and religious education. She feels she is in a better position to do this because she invests much more time in the children and knows more about children's issues than her husband does. Her husband doesn't feel this is fair because he believes that the children are as much his as hers.

Both spouses are using the exact same justifications to buttress their position: they earned the right to make the majority of the decisions because they've worked harder on the issue than the other spouse and know more about the issues under discussion. Yet, each denies the validity of the other's justifications. This is a typical impasse that needs to be negotiated according to principles of justice that don't change from one spouse to the other.

Other typical situations involving money occur when both partners work. The concept of "my money" and "your money" can enter the picture. If we can't afford to buy an antique clock out of the general household funds, then I'll buy it with "my money." The justice issue that arises here is: Does each spouse get an equal allowance, regardless of their incomes, or are their allowances proportionate to their incomes? The former situation will likely cause more justice conflicts than the latter.

Another typical situation involves a spouse receiving gift money, for example, from his or her parents on a birthday. Is this the recipient's private money to do with as he or she chooses, or does it go into the general fund?

Because couples rarely face these issues before marriage, even when they live with each other, this area can be one of sudden and unexpected conflict. Therefore, it's helpful to discuss the possible situations that can arise before marriage.

Work

Distribution of work is another area in which justice issues arise. Marriages in which the word "work" is reserved only for a salaried job are especially likely to have problems in this area. For example, the husband "works" all day, comes home exhausted, and feels he has earned the right to rest until the next morning. When his wife asks him to feed the children, help half of them with their homework, and repair the sink, he clearly feels that this is unfair.

On the other hand, his balking at these requests for help are perceived as unfair by his wife. It is true, she only "works" twenty hours a week, but she also gets the children up, feeds them, drives them to school, picks them up after school, drives them to each of their after–school activities, shops for the family, cooks all the meals, washes and dries the dishes, helps half the kids with their homework, and gets all of them ready for bed. On any "exhaustion meter," she registers at least the same degree of exhaustion as her husband at the end of the day. Her work is no more stimulating than his, and her rewards no greater.

Until the concept of "work" can be extended to include any stressful and fatiguing activity done for the sake of the family, justice conflicts are likely to arise.

Freedom

Freedom is another issue that involves justice issues. Who takes, or is allowed, more freedom? Traditionally, husbands have had more freedom—to change jobs, to go out with "the boys," to decide when the family vacation will be, to take an evening course, to go away with fishing partners for the weekend. On the other hand, wives more or less stayed at home and didn't think much about freedom for themselves.

Today more women are likely to want the same freedoms

as their husbands. They want the freedom to work or return to school, to go out with friends for an evening, or to visit friends over a weekend. Their feeling is that they have the same rights to and needs for free time and free choice that their husbands have.

When husbands agree with their wives, no justice conflicts will ensue. But if husbands believe that freedom is their right but not their wife's as well, justice conflicts are likely to arise.

A variation of this problem occurs if a wife feels she does not need or desire the kinds of freedom that her husband does. She is perfectly content staying home seven nights a week and can't understand why her husband has to go out. In other words, because she doesn't need certain kinds of freedom, she uses this to deny freedom to her husband ("What's wrong with us that you need to go out and get your needs met with other people?"). Here again, a justice issue arises that will be dealt with either constructively or destructively, depending on the motives and skills of the couple.

Partners in marriage frequently will protest that something isn't fair. Sometimes they will be right—it isn't fair, and negotiations must take place to make the situation more fair. At other times, they will be correct, and nothing can be done about it. For example, a couple may have to move right after the wife has found a job she loves because her husband got transferred. It's not fair, but if the family's survival is largely dependent on the husband's income and career advancement, the move may have to be made. In other words, sometimes things are unfair, and people must respond as well as they can.

Sometimes, a husband or wife will think that something is unfair, but he or she will be incorrect. Partners must realize that, although they may not like a situation, it's not necessarily unfair. It may be eminently fair but not pleasant to accept. Finally, it's appropriate for partners to be at least mildly vigilant about becoming the victims of injustice, but it is equally important to be vigilant that they do not foist injustice on their partner. In other words, I should be as willing to examine the fairness of my behavior toward you as I am to examine the fairness of your behavior toward me.

Questions for Thought and Discussion

1. I think I'm not always fair with my partner. For example, sometimes I

_____

_____.

2. When I am unfair, my partner typically reacts by

_____

_____.

3. My partner does not always treat me fairly. For example,

_____

_____.

4. When my partner treats me unfairly, I typically react by

_____

_____.

Disappointment

Many institutions in life have unrealistic expectations attached to them, and marriage certainly ranks among the top. People's perception of marriage is almost schizophrenic. The pessimistic view is that marriages rarely seem to work out and even people who remain married don't seem that happy ("How many married couples do *you* know that are genuinely happy?"). The optimistic view is that although many married people are obviously unhappy, *we know* we won't be one of them because *we* know what we're doing. Marriage for us will be great.

As with most realities, the reality of marriage lies someplace between the most optimistic and the most pessimistic perceptions. Disappointments usually begin to occur after the honeymoon period, when the routine and stresses of everyday living peel off the final layers of the couple's dating personalities. Each partner thought that the other was more mature, selfless, realistic, industrious, wise, secure, loving, fair, patient, reasonable, honest, or even-tempered than he or she turned out to be.

Disappointments, however, aren't limited to your partner. You can be disappointed with yourself. After partners are tested through the first year or two of marriage, they often find that they've let themselves down. A partner may have always thought that marriage would only bring out the best in him or her—that he or she would be totally loving, giving, and patient and would never be concerned about such petty considerations as who's turn it is to put out the garbage or to get up with the baby. In fact, sometimes disappointment with your partner covers up a deeper disappointment with yourself. Instead of saying that I'm disappointed with how impatient I am with my husband, I blame him for being impatient with my impatience.

Disappointments can also be connected to parenthood, even with the first baby. Deep down, one or both spouses wanted a baby with blond rather than brown hair, or blue eyes instead of hazel, or fair skin instead of darker skin. They wanted a relaxed baby and got a fretful one; wished for a friendly baby and got a detached one.

The partners thought that they'd be more patient with their baby, more relaxed, selfless, warm, and happy than they find themselves to be. They feel guilty and ashamed that the baby's crying irritates them, that they resent attending to the baby in the middle of the night, and that they become infuriated when the baby spits out food or soils clothes.

Couples can even become disappointed with the institutions of marriage and parenthood. Because marriage means the lifelong commitment of two people deeply in love, it should bring out only the best in them, but they find it also brings out the worst. They've never loved so much and felt so secure, but they've never hated so much and felt so insecure. They discover that marriage doesn't work for them—they must work for their marriage.

Because parenthood is a supreme gift, it should evoke all the warmth, affection, and patience that a parent has, which it does. But it also evokes the parents' impatience, frustration, and helplessness.

The main thing is to expect any and all of these disappointments because it's quite possible, if not likely, that they will occur. But it's also important to place these disappointments in a proper light and deal with them in a helpful way.

Disappointment should be seen as a normal and natural part of marriage and parenthood and should not be made to mean more than it does. When my wife disappoints me, it doesn't necessarily mean that she is "not as good as I thought," because, in some ways, she may be better. Nor does it necessarily mean that she is just letting her hair down and being the selfish person she always was but successfully hid from me until she finally got me to marry her. All it may mean is that she's not as perfect as I made her out to be, or as perfect as she would dearly like to be and hoped that she could be for me. If people were perfect, there would be no need for them to marry and work toward completion. The same flaws that cause disappointment are the ones that, when worked upon, form the foundation for a strong, enduring marriage.

When dealing with disappointment, it's good to remember that we're probably "letting down" our partner and ourselves as much if not more than our partner is letting us down. Therefore, instead of being "let down," "surprised," or "shocked" by a partner's flaws, it's more helpful to discuss the issue at hand. For example, if you're not as patient with me as you were when we were dating, I might say: "You know, both of us are going to have to continue making adjustments to each other. I think sometimes you could be a little more patient with me, and I'm sure I could be more helpful to you in one or two ways. Can we talk about this so we can get rid of the molehills before they become mountains?" This type of dialogue avoids emotionally laden terms and facilitates the mutual growth process.

Questions for Thought and Discussion

1. Some things that make me feel disappointed in our relationship are

   _____

   _____ .

2. When I'm disappointed, I tend to

   _____

   _____ .

3. To be honest, I have to admit that I know I disappoint my partner because

   _____

   _____ .

4. When disappointed, my partner tends to react by

   _____

   _____ .

Summary

Most, if not all, marriages have periods of boredom, feeling used, suffering, and injustice. Sometimes these experiences are mild and short-lived, and at other times they are acute and of longer duration. In themselves, they do not present a reason to question the goodness of the partners or the health of the marriage. All of these feelings and experiences can be used to strengthen the character of both the spouses and their marriage. It is only when one or more of these experiences becomes acute and is not dealt with constructively that serious damage can be done, both to the spouses as individuals and to their marriage and parenthood.

APPENDIX A

Working with Your Minister

Many couples who plan to marry will meet with their minister as part of the preparation for their wedding and marriage. Some couples do so because they want to get some psychological and spiritual input. They realize that they are embarking on a serious journey into unexplored territory and want to be as prepared as possible for it. Other couples meet with their minister because they want a Christian wedding, and this requires them to go through a marriage preparation program. Some of these couples may look forward to this program as an opportunity to learn more about themselves and their relationship, while others view it as a needless exercise—as just another "hoop" they must jump through in order to get married.

Whatever your reasons for meeting with a minister, it can be helpful to approach the situation in an informed manner so that you can get the most out of this important time. Here are some issues that you and your partner can discuss with each other and with the minister so that you will find the experience most beneficial.

Who Is Your Minister?

Ministers are as different from one another as members of any profession—doctors, lawyers, teachers, or architects—are different. However, they tend to have some characteristics in common.

First, they believe that a Christian marriage can provide a wealth of meaning, strength, support, counsel, and grace that will enrich marriage and parenthood with an abiding sense of love, security, and reward.

Second, they have, by virtue of their education, training, and life experiences, convinced academic and church authorities that they are competent to counsel people in areas such as marriage preparation.

Third, they take the institution of marriage very seriously and want to do all in their power to help couples approach it with realistic confidence and sound competencies.

And finally, they are human beings and, as such, at times will be too intrusive, boring, opinionated, tired, detached, or nondirective—again, just like doctors, lawyers, teachers, or architects. Just like you and me. But it's important not to allow your minister's humanity to distract or discourage you from all that he or she has to offer.

Questions to Ask Your Minister

All couples who plan to meet with their minister for marriage preparation will have questions. The following are some typical questions couples raise.

Will a male minister be able to understand the woman's needs, values, and hopes regarding marriage and motherhood?

Will a female minister be able to understand the man's motivations, priorities, and expectations regarding marriage and fatherhood?

Will a single, celibate minister be able to counsel about marriage, sexuality, and parenthood if he or she has never experienced any of these things?

Will a newly ordained minister possess the experience and wisdom to offer us any more help than our friends already have offered?

Will a minister who comes from a different ethnic background be able to understand our situation?

Will a much older minister be sufficiently familiar with the issues facing young adults today and be able to help us deal with them?

Will a minister try to brainwash us with his or her opinions and not respect our opinions when they are different?

Will the minister always meet with us together as a couple, or will she or he also want to see us separately?

If one of us is of a different religion than the minister, will he or she try to convert us?

If one or both of us can't relate to the minister, can we ask to see another one?

Is it all right to disagree openly with the minister?

How can we feel comfortable talking about sexual issues with a minister?

What if one (or both) of us doesn't agree with the church's teachings on a particular issue related to marriage or parenthood? Should we discuss this? Can we still get married in the church?

What if the minister thinks we should postpone our wedding? What then?

What about confidentiality? Will our discussions be held in confidence, or will the minister, directly or indirectly, communicate what we discuss with others?

Each one of these questions is legitimate and, when they are an issue, should be discussed with your partner and the minister. Ministers want to do everything possible to make your visits comfortable and worthwhile. Therefore, they will welcome your questions and view them as honest attempts on your part to "clear the air" so that the three of you can work together in an open and trusting relationship. It would not be helpful to withhold reservations or doubts, thereby allowing them to shortcircuit communication, cooperation, and trust. When doubts are not aired and laid to rest, it almost ensures that the experience will be a waste of time.

A word about religion. Some people who consult with a minister are actively religious, and their visits will simply be a logical extension of their life up to that point in time. Other people are passively religious; that is, they've had some religious upbringing and believe in God but are not active in their religion and/or church. Still others have little or no interest in religion or are antagonistic toward it.

It is fairly common for one partner to have an attitude toward religion that the other does not share. If this is the case, the couple needs to take a close look at this discrepancy, especially if religion is a basic value to one partner but only a superficial or negative value to the other. A discrepancy in this area can be the source of significant conflict in marriage once the honeymoon period is over.

During marriage preparation, any of these situations can be discussed with the minister. Ministers are used to working with people who disagree with them or with the principles they uphold. Both you and your minister may learn something important in an honest and constructive exchange of ideas.

Questions to Ask Yourself

In addition to questions that may arise about your minister, here are some equally important questions you can ask yourselves.

What do you, *personally*, want to receive from the visits with your minister? Does what you want coincide with what your partner wants, or is there some discrepancy?

Why do you want a church wedding? Is it a natural extension of your religious commitment? Is it because a religious ceremony will make you feel more married than a ceremony before a judge or justice of the peace? Is it because your parents want you to get married in the church?

Are you looking forward to the visits with your minister as an opportunity to learn something about yourself, your relationship, and marriage as an institution, or is it just another requirement to meet in order to get married?

Are you willing to be open and honest about yourself, your partner, and your relationship with your minister, or are you planning to be selective in what you discuss?

What reservations or reluctance do you have about going through with the marriage preparation process?

Do you view the visits as isolated events or as stimuli that will engender a good deal of discussion between you and your partner outside of the sessions as well?

Honest answers to these questions before you visit with your minister can prepare the way for a very beneficial series of visits.

Issues to Discuss with Your Minister

Sometimes couples wonder what they should discuss with their minister. Some couples have a great deal to discuss, but they wonder what's appropriate, what's too personal, or what a minister can actually do to help. Other couples feel that they don't have anything significant to say to a minister. They meet with the minister because it's required in order to have a church wedding.

Therefore, it may be helpful to consider some issues that couples often find beneficial to discuss with their minister as they approach marriage. All these issues can be examined under the concept of intimacy because intimacy is at the heart of a marriage relationship. As you consider these issues, it will be helpful to keep in mind that striving toward perfection is a lifelong goal of marriage. You can't expect to be perfect or to have a perfect relationship at this point. The question you should be asking yourself is not "Are we a perfect couple?" but "In what areas would I like to see us grow so that we can continue to develop in the direction of perfection?"

Intimacy means being close. People can be close in these areas:

Physical

Physical intimacy includes both sexual and nonsexual closeness. For many people, nonsexual physical intimacy (embracing, kissing, hand-holding, stroking, or snuggling that is not erotic) is as important or more important than sexual physical intimacy.

Sexual intimacy refers not only to sexual intercourse but to all erotic physical behavior that not only leads to but continues after sexual intercourse.

What are your feelings about nonsexual and sexual physical intimacy in your relationship? In what areas do you feel quite satisfied and in what areas are you less than satisfied?

Intellectual

Intellectual intimacy refers to how much a couple openly and constructively share their thoughts, beliefs, values, doubts, and hopes with each other. Some people are very intellectually honest. They operate on the principle "Who you see is who you get." Others are very open but express their ideas in destructive ways that put down, ridicule, or hurt others. Some couples are selective about the thoughts they share, choosing to censor those that may create personal or interpersonal tension. Still others don't share many of their private thoughts at all.

How satisfied are you with the intellectual intimacy of your relationship? Which parts do you feel very good about, and which need more work?

Emotional

Emotional intimacy refers to how openly and constructively a couple share feelings (in contrast to thoughts) with each other. How well do they express hurt, warmth, fear, compassion, sadness, joy, doubt, trust, anger, gratitude, shame, pride, despair, and hope?

Some people express their feelings in open and constructive ways that clarify and strengthen a relationship. Others express feelings in open but destructive ways that confuse and weaken a relationship. Still others keep a tight rein on their feelings, choosing to keep them to themselves.

What is your view of emotional intimacy in your relationship? Is it at a level that makes you feel very comfortable, or do you wish things were a little better?

Social

Social intimacy refers to how comfortably couples relate to each other privately and publicly. Some couples are very comfortable with each other, both in private and in public. They respect each other, are sensitive to each other's needs, can offer and receive constructive criticism, can be spontaneous and free, and enjoy each other's company.

Some couples relate well with each other in private but tend to ignore or argue with each other in public, while other couples tend to ignore or argue with each other in private but get along well in public, at least superficially.

Still other couples feel comfortable with each other only when there is a third party present or when they are doing a project together. When there is "no one around" or "nothing to do," they are uncomfortable (bored, tense, irritable) with each other.

How do you feel about social intimacy in your relationship? Do you feel it's right where it should be, given the duration of your relationship, or would you like to see growth occur in some areas?

Spiritual

Spiritual intimacy refers to how well a couple share their souls. This means how much they share their thoughts and feelings about the meaning of life, about what constitutes good (right) and bad (wrong) behavior, about afterlife, and about religious beliefs and practices.

Some people have a well-integrated spirituality that may or may not include a formal religious element. Other people are striving toward an integrated spirituality but experience periods of confusion and doubt. Still others are not at all conversant with, or caring about, things other than the material.

Some people have a strong religious faith and practice it. Some are religious but don't attend church. Others are not religious, and still others are antagonistic toward religion.

How satisfied are you with the spiritual side of your relationship? Do you feel quite close to each other spiritually, or do you feel concern, disappointment, or tension in this area?

This, of course, is only a snapshot of what intimacy entails. In a sense, this entire book is about intimacy in a love relationship. But the hope is that being aware of the basic elements of intimacy will provide you with some thoughts and feelings to discuss with your minister, along with any other ideas, questions, or doubts you may have about yourself and/or your relationship.

You may also be interested in reading Appendix B, which discusses some of the things your minister will do to help you. The more each of you know about the other's motives and roles, the more helpful you can be to each other.

APPENDIX   B

How Ministers Can Help Couples

It is important for ministers to have a deep appreciation of the opportunity they have to touch the lives of couples preparing for marriage. Couples who are planning to marry often are at a critical point in their lives. They are letting go of many needs, interests, attachments, and relationships of their youth, but have not yet replaced them with the joys, sorrows, and commitment of marriage and parenthood.

Because these couples are in a transitional state and facing uncharted waters (marriage and parenthood), they are often at a reachable and teachable stage. Spiritually, many have outgrown the religion of their youth, yet they have had little opportunity to replace it with a mature religion. Because the Christian theology of love, marriage, and parenthood is, in many ways, a microcosm of Christianity, marriage preparation may be the first and last opportunity to offer the couple private tutoring in a mature Christian faith. The marriage preparation that ministers provide is likely to be the only marriage preparation that couples receive. Therefore, it takes on great and lasting importance, both psychologically and spiritually.

This section deals with seven points that ministers can be mindful of as they grow in their effectiveness to help couples prepare for a lifelong marriage.

1. *When conflicts arise in a relationship, it is rare, despite outward appearances, for one partner to be the innocent victim and the other the sole perpetrator.*

For example, Margaret loves Jim very much but has expressed concern about his drinking. When Jim drinks, he embarrasses her, says hurtful things, and drives when he shouldn't. As the minister delves sensitively but thoroughly into the situation, the following dynamics may be discovered.

Margaret knows, at least on some level of consciousness, that when she becomes extremely critical and demanding of Jim, he is likely to drink too much to exert his independence and to get back at her. Even though she knows this, she does nothing to modify her behavior. This is not to imply it is her fault that Jim drinks—only that she doesn't go out of her way to help him in this regard.

Though on one level she hates it when Jim drinks too much, on another, two factors give her a vested interest in his drinking. First, she has a deep-seated discomfort about her sexuality, and when Jim is drinking, she refuses to have anything to do with him, thus excusing herself from having to admit and deal with her own discomfort.

The second reason is that she has some deep feelings of inadequacy, especially with respect to men. When Jim drinks, it allows her to feel in control of the situation and remain blameless if anything goes wrong in their relationship.

When Jim is drinking and "cute about it," Margaret laughs at his antics, drives him home from parties, and helps to hide his misbehavior from his parents. So, while on the one hand, Margaret is genuinely concerned about Jim's drinking, she not only fails to deliver an ultimatum prohibiting it but tacitly rewards him for doing it.

It is important for ministers who are helping a couple examine their conflicts to also help them recognize that "it takes two to tango." Consequently, for problematic behaviors to change, each partner is likely to have to change at least one significant thing about his or her behavior.

Most ministers will not get deeply involved in this area, but it's important that they be aware of such dynamics so that they can respond in an enlightened manner when they encounter them in couples about to be married.

2. *If a couple is very insecure, they are more likely to attempt to manipulate the sessions to keep the minister from getting a fully accurate picture of their relationship. This manipulation can take several forms.*

A couple may appear very nice, friendly, and cooperative—"a great couple to work with." The problem arises when the minister gets so focused on the perceived sweetness of their relationship that he or she fails to challenge them in the areas of fear, confusion, insecurity, anger, and ambivalence that lie close to the heart of their relationship. The couple has won a fan rather than engaged a minister.

A couple can be so issue-centered that the minister remains stuck in the role of educator and neglects to fulfill the role of counselor. The couple does this by expressing serious interest in the theological, ecclesial, and administrative parts of the wedding and marriage—so much interest that there is no time to focus on the psychospiritual dynamics of their relationship.

Some couples assume at least a mildly adversarial stance toward the minister. They present endless whys, and challenge the minister at every turn. A minister who is on the defensive can't learn much about the couple. In effect, it is the minister and the church that is being examined and discussed, not the couple's relationship.

A couple can be so unreliable in their approach to marriage preparation that they leave the minister little time, energy, or motivation to work with them in areas that need work. They forget appointments, arrive late, fail to do their homework, and are inattentive during the sessions. This wears down and frustrates the minister to the point that he or she just wants to get the wedding over with and move on to more rewarding endeavors.

Couples can avoid talking about issues they are uncomfortable with that should be examined and discussed. They do this by shifting the focus of the questions they are asked. For example, a minister might ask, "Well, Bill, have you seen any changes in your relationship since we've been meeting?" Bill answers, "Definitely. Both of us understand much more about what a Christian marriage entails than we did before we came in here." This *sounds* as if Bill is answering the question, but he isn't. His response sheds no light on how their *relationship* has been affected by the visits with the minister.

None of these manipulative ploys is necessarily conscious. Each is usually a subliminal defense that the people have adopted years before they met. But regardless of how unconscious it is, ministers must be able to detect manipulation and overcome it to be of genuine help to couples.

3. *All couples relate on varying levels of awareness or consciousness.*

In healthy relationships, unconscious dynamics will be minimized; however, few relationships are totally devoid of unconscious dynamics and they need to be examined. Typically, issues that are relegated to the unconscious include thoughts, feelings, and motives that conflict with a person's self-concept. For example, Al might view himself as a self-sufficient, secure, and liberating individual, even though deep down, he is quite dependent, insecure, and possessive. As long as Sandy is with him and sharing her love with him, he feels on top of the world. However, when Sandy wants to spend time with her family or friends, Al becomes sullen and critical. According to his view, it's fine if Sandy wants to be with other people. It's just that he feels her parents are very domineering and her friends are immature; in addition, Sandy always waits until the last minute to inform him of her plans. Of course, he gets upset. Who wouldn't?

Sandy views herself as a sensitive, gentle person, but deep down, she has a cruel streak that often surfaces when she is hurt. When Al says to her, "I can't believe you're going out again with your friends," Sandy responds, "Well, at least I've got some friends to go out with, and I don't have to sit at home alone feeling sorry for myself because there's nothing else to do." Neither Al nor Sandy understands the dynamics at work in their relationship. Al sees the problem as Sandy's choice of friends, while Sandy thinks Al's jealousy is the problem.

Until Al can understand, accept, and work on his unconscious insecurities, his behavior will remain destructive whenever Sandy wants to spend time with anyone else. And until Sandy can recognize, accept, and work on controlling the anger that she unleashes when she is hurt, she will do great damage in the relationship.

A trained minister will recognize that when a negative behavior "comes out of the blue," "makes no sense," "just wasn't me," or is more intense than the situation merits, it is likely that unconscious factors are at work.

4. *Each individual and every couple is unique.*

Although no one would debate this concept in principle, it often is overlooked in practice. Three mistakes, in particular, often occur in pre-wedding sessions with a minister.

First, a minister may attempt to apply to the wrong couple a principle learned from a book or a workshop. For example, a minister who has learned that it's good for people to air their feelings may take this as an absolute principle: It's always good for all people under all circumstances to get their feelings out. Having correctly observed that Fred and Ava share a very intellectual relationship, the minister confronts them on this issue, names some emotional issues that they *must* have some deep feelings about, and asks them to discuss them before their next visit. This technique has two problems: Neither Fred nor Ava is ready to share feelings about these issues and neither has the skills to express feelings in a way that assures a positive outcome. Consequently, these attempts to discuss emotional issues leave them with deep feelings of inadequacy, frustration, and embarrassment, which gets recycled into distrust or anger toward the minister.

Second, some ministers mistakenly assume that what worked with one couple will work with all couples, especially in similar situations. For example, a minister might suggest that a couple refrain from romantic and sexual behaviors for a week to concentrate on all the other beautiful things in their relationship. The couple does this and reports that it was very helpful. Because of this success, the minister advises the next couple he sees to try the same thing. However, after three days of this, they decide to find a minister who is "more real." To be effective, ministers must allow sufficient time to get to know a couple's needs before recommending particular techniques to deal with them.

Third, a minister may make the mistake of operating on the "if I were you" principle. For example, a minister will tell a couple, "If I were you, I'd sit down with both sets of parents and very nicely state how I feel, so that everyone will know exactly where I stand before the marriage."

This approach has three problems: (1) the minister is not the couple; (2) the minister's parents are not the couple's parents; (3) the minister does not have to live with the consequences of that advice.

Rather than assuming he already knows the couple's position on various issues, it would be better to ask questions that allow them to reveal it. "Well, what do *you* think would be the best approach with regard to your parents?" or "If you were advising a couple in the same situation you're in, what would you think they should do?" Questions like these keep the focus on the couple and their situation—questions to which only they have answers.

5. *It is a normal part of human nature to be ambivalent about psychological intimacy.*

As couples grow more intimate, the opportunity increases for them to experience not only beautiful things but also hurtful ones. The normal pursuit of intimacy may be compared to the approach-avoidance behavior of children at a beach on a hot day. They run pell-mell toward the cool water, but as soon as they feel how cold it is, they quickly retreat to the warmer land. Therefore, it's important for both ministers and couples to be alert to approach-avoidance behavior not only during courtship but throughout marriage.

Although common in intimate relationships, not all approach-avoidance behaviors fall within a tolerable range. In at least four situations approach-avoidance behaviors can create inordinate tension in a relationship. In the first, one partner understands and values intimacy, while the other, lacking this knowledge and appreciation, perhaps views sexual intercourse as the sum total of the meaning of intimacy.

A second situation involves chronic desynchronization in the closeness-distance dynamics of the couple; that is, each time one partner indicates a desire for closeness, the other rejects it.

Third, intimacy can be used as a bargaining chip in a relationship. One partner, for example, may negotiate: "I'll give you intimacy if you give me the freedom I need"; or threaten: "If you continue to upset me, I'll withdraw from you until you get the message."

A fourth damaging situation is when one or both partners desire intimacy on a conscious level but, unconsciously, have an inordinate fear of it. So each partner (or just one) welcomes intimacy with one hand but pushes it away with the other, often by picking a fight about something out of the blue in order to create distance in the relationship when the other gets too close.

When any of these dynamics is present in a relationship, significant tensions will arise. Ministers can point out to couples the normal ambivalence all human beings have toward psychological intimacy and help them understand and deal with it; it should not be assumed, however, that all ambivalence toward intimacy is normal. Significant conflicts over intimacy issues can do great damage to a relationship and should be addressed with appropriate concern.

6. *People are rarely helped by advice.*

Here are a few of the reasons that those in ministry are so greatly inclined to give advice:

It is easier to give a couple advice than it is to help them learn to solve their own problems.

People view ministers as advice-givers (as they do most helping professionals). The first thing many people say to a minister is "I've got a problem. What should I do?"

When ministers give advice, it makes them feel they've

done something for the couple, and the couple reinforces this feeling by telling the minister that he's been very helpful.

People *want* advice from ministers because it frees them from doing their own thinking and accepting full responsibility for their decisions.

And, finally, ministers give advice because they themselves have too often been raised on a steady diet of advice.

Despite the strong motivation for ministers to give advice on specific personal matters, it is rarely helpful except on a short-term, superficial level. This is because receiving advice preempts the couple's decision-making process.

Ordinarily, the role of ministers in marriage preparation is not to give advice on personal or relationship issues (as opposed to giving advice about appropriate music for the wedding, for instance). When couples have a problem making their own decisions, ministers can help them develop a methodology for problem solving. Here is a sample of what is meant by a methodology:

1. Define the problem clearly.

2. List *all* possible solutions.

3. Examine *all* the consequences of each possible solution.

4. Measure the consequences of each possible solution against those of the other solutions.

5. Try the solution that appears to be the best, and, if it works, the problem is solved; if it doesn't, try the next-best solution on the list.

6. When a solution works, learn from the situation in order to prevent similar problems in the future.

7. Know that the more complicated a problem is, the less ideal the solution is likely to be. Be prepared to accept lesser-of-the-evils solutions, as well as partial solutions.

8. Understand that not all problems are solvable, but most problems can be accommodated if the desire is there.

Counseling in this manner takes more time, energy, and patience than simply giving advice to a couple, which usually takes less than ten minutes on even the most complicated issues. However, couples about to marry need procedures they can use to find their own answers; they don't need the answers that ministers would find correct for themselves if they were in the same situation.

7. *Many problems that couples reveal to ministers, even though commonplace, are not simple.*

Effective ministers realize the seriousness of problems discussed and avoid offering simplistic solutions. They know that advice of the kind listed below is ordinarily ineffective:

To tell a couple who argue a lot that they just need to be more patient with each other.

To tell a selfish couple that they need to be more sensitive to the needs of the other and be willing to sacrifice for each other.

To tell couples who have different needs and values that they must learn to compromise. (If she wants two children and he wants one, how do they compromise?)

To tell a couple anxious about sexuality that they shouldn't worry because everything will fall into place after the marriage.

To tell couples that their premarital jitters are normal and not to give them a second thought.

To tell a couple who are having problems communicating that they should set aside a certain time each week and just talk.

To tell a couple with a drinking problem that they need to set limits on their drinking and be aware of how drinking can hurt them and their relationship.

To tell a couple experiencing difficulties that things will be fine as soon as they settle down and have a baby.

This list constitutes a Band-Aid approach to marriage preparation, and, as is true of Band-Aids, they will fall off in a few days, or worse yet, infect the wound they're intended to heal.

In all likelihood, each of the situations described above needs more serious attention than the minister gives it. This does not mean that ministers must delve into the depths of the couple's souls; the minister may lack the time, competence, and/or motivation to do so. Nevertheless, ministers have a duty to do something between simply offering a Band-Aid, which anyone can do, and performing major surgery, which only a skilled practitioner should attempt. They can at least help a couple get a clearer picture of the nature and extent of their difficulty. When appropriate, the minister can make a referral to another minister or counselor who can follow up on the situation.

It also may be helpful for ministers to read Appendix A (Working with Your Minister) to be reminded of the questions and concerns couples typically have as they approach marriage preparation visits. Being able to anticipate these issues and deal with them if they arise can be very helpful in facilitating the marriage preparation process.

DATE DUE

GAYLORD   PRINTED IN U.S.A